MY FAITH *Journey*

FROM RITUAL TO RELATIONSHIP

MARGARET A. KOBIER

BALBOA.PRESS

A DIVISION OF HAY HOUSE

Balboa Press books may be ordered through booksellers or by contacting:

Balboa Press
A Division of Hay House
1663 Liberty Drive
Bloomington, IN 47403
www.balboapress.com.au
AU TFN: 1 800 844 925 (Toll Free inside Australia)
AU Local: 0283 107 086 (+61 2 8310 7086 from outside Australia)

Scripture taken from the King James Version of the Bible.

Print information available on the last page.

ISBN: 978-1-5043-2327-7 (sc)
ISBN: 978-1-5043-2328-4 (e)

Balboa Press rev. date: 12/11/2020

Thy word is a lamp unto my feet, and a light unto my path. (Psalm 119.105)

* * *

These (the people from Berea) were more noble than those in Thessalonica, in that they received the word with all readiness of mind, and searched the scriptures daily, whether those things were so. (Acts 17:11)

PREFACE

AS WE GET older, many of us take a journey back through our lives looking at the highs and lows, rediscovering childhood stamping grounds and facing more openly the questions of life, religion and even politics. While many questions may not be answered clearly in this life, we can gain new perspectives and even respond to situations in a different and more confident way as we continue to learn and grow in maturity and hopefully, wisdom.

My story is not intended to disparage the Catholic Church or anyone who shares this faith. My conclusions to date may not be theologically sound according to many. However, this is the sharing of my personal journey through what I saw were conflicting and unsubstantiated beliefs that stood out as I moved through my life. There is a saying that 'God has no grandchildren'. Each one of us has this journey to undertake to find Him for ourselves.

My questioning may be helpful or even encouraging to others who have questions of their own and are hesitant to look for answers.

MY JOURNEY TO and with God our amazing Creator began in a Catholic family in a small country town in Australia

WE LIVED IN a small country town where I went through my schooling and education until after finishing Year 3 high school (roughy equivalent to Yr 10 now) and then moved to a bigger town with more opportunities. This small country town was like many others in the 1950's. The townsfolk provided the support and services required by the farmers producing wheat and sheep in the surrounding area. The 'country' kids travelled to school by bus and had the amazing privilege of eating sandwiches for lunch while the 'town' kids, like me, mostly had to go home at lunchtime (if you lived reasonably close to the schools) for lunch which was, for us, the main meal of the day. If my Dad was working locally, he would come home for lunch and then go back to work as we went back to school.

CHURCH and family intertwined

RELIGION PLAYED AN important part in our childhood. Most folks were either Catholic or Protestant or Church of England though the latter two seemed to be interchangeable as to my child's mind a person was either Catholic or Protestant.

Belonging to the Catholic Church was far more than being part of a religion. It gave one a sense of community and of belonging and no matter in which town one went to Mass, there was that connection with others through the same sequence of prayer, scripture readings, homily, the Offertory, Consecration, Communion and Final Blessing. In later years I found this same continuity overseas even if the language was not my own. It was familiar no matter where we went. This provided community and connection.

There were two schools in the town, the Catholic School and the Public School with many a childhood dirt clod/rock throwing 'war' between the 'Cathos' and the 'Prodos'. That was about as divisive as I ever remember it.

Businesses worked throughout the week with shops closing at 1pm on Saturdays til Monday morning. Sundays were classed as days of rest though the football players got a work out on the footy field on Sunday afternoons.

MY PARENTS

MY MUM WAS Catholic and my Dad was from an Anglican background. He converted to Catholicism to marry mum. At that time, marrying a non Catholic was a big 'No. No' and whether it was that or something else, I, around the age of 10, became aware that he had been reluctantly accepted into the family.

Mum's family would be classed Irish Catholic with strict religious boundaries governing all areas of life yet I saw contradictions. There were several occasions when actions did not match the religiosity. I didn't dare question and I had a hard enough time interpreting what I was been taught and how to apply the contradictions to my good, or more often, bad behaviour.

MY FAVOURITE AND precious memory of my Dad was his morning prayer. He would stand near the water heater, close his eyes, clasp his hands and quietly talk to God. One could tug on his trouser leg to try to get his attention but when he was saying his morning prayers, nothing interrupted those few minutes. Mum told me of an occasion when Dad had gone out with his army mates and was brought home drunk. Before going to bed, he knelt down and said his prayers.

MY MUM WAS very much into attending all Church happenings and the daily family Rosary. Both Mum and Dad taught me different aspects of God and His Son Jesus. For this I am very very thankful.

The dispenser of discipline in our home was our mum. This was partly because she was mainly in the home while Dad went out to work and occasionally, when there was no local work, away to live and work. So Mum set the rules and obedience was the key. I didn't like being disciplined, usually by the strap, and like many a child would say I 'copped it' when it was someone else's fault. I remember Pop's razor strop hanging near the door. I think my uncle's felt that from time to time.

DAD'S HEALTH WASN'T the best from about his late 50's due to the various types of work he undertook and the smoking. He was now unable to work full time and occupied himself with a variety of odd jobs which enabled him to contribute to and help people around him and earn a few dollars.

THERE WAS A spot outside the back door where my dad liked to sit. I could wander out and ask 'Whatcha up to Dad?' His response was often 'Just talking to Jesus and Mary'. His daily ongoing relationship with Jesus gave me a different view of interaction with God to that of the ritual attendance training given by Mum. Dad showed me that God was real outside the church and one didn't have to 'go to' church to connect with Him. I don't think I consciously thought about this but just absorbed it and, in a way, lived it. Later on Mum would share her increased knowledge of God working in our daily life and that was, for me, another step along the path of faith.

ON OCCASION, I would talk to dad about praying for something. His reply was along the lines of 'We don't need to bother God with the little things'. This puzzled me because I thought it was good to talk to God about everything - the big and little. Yet, in a way, I can agree with Dad on this. We don't need to bother God with the 'little things' because He is pre-prepared and often has things in place to preempt our needs but like a loving father, He wants us to come to Him with our daily needs. In His teaching on prayer, Jesus taught us to pray:

> *"After this manner therefore pray ye: Our Father which art in heaven, Hallowed be thy name. Thy kingdom come. Thy will be done in earth, as it is in heaven. Give us this day our daily bread. And forgive us our debts, as we forgive our debtors. And lead us not into temptation, but deliver us from evil: For thine is the kingdom, and the power, and the glory, for ever. Amen." (Matthew 6:9-13)*

LOVE

IT IS INTERESTING to realise as an adult the different ways my parents expressed love. My Mum loved through the doing: washing, cleaning, cooking, etc but Dad was the one we went to for cuddles. Sitting on his knee and rubbing his bald head while he sang 'Two Little Girls In Blue' or 'Kiss Me Goodnight Sergeant Major' was always a special time.

IT WASN'T UNTIL I was an adult that I realised that giving Mum a kiss was not a natural happening and I consciously worked at acknowledging her with a kiss. Despite the lack of physical touch with Mum, she was always the one I wanted to share life's happenings with including the challenges with individual children. She could always be relied upon to pray for the person or situation and together, at times, share faith. Even now, years after her death, I find myself thinking 'I must tell mum ...'

WHERE DO I sit on the love spectrum? That's an interesting thought. I love touch so hugs are a must but I also like assistance with doing things even when I know I can do it myself. There is something special about 'Can I help you with that?'

I like to help other people to do things or listen to their story (though it's hard not to butt in with advice) and have a sense of being unwanted or unneeded when I do not have the opportunity to interact with others in helpful ways whether physical assistance or providing an ear.

Our Father Who Art in heaven (and who helps us here on earth)

IN MY OWN JOURNEY, I have found my Heavenly Father to be very aware of the 'little things' in an ongoing way and often I have found that He knew what my needs, sometimes big ones, would be in advance and would have already, even months earlier, set in place the exact answer to my need.

ONE EXAMPLE OF provision in the 'little things' is the path replacement project.

I had decided to improve the safety of the path across the back yard. The path comprised 400x400 cement pavers placed unevenly through the weed and plant growth. The work was hastened by the need to put in drainage to deal with storm water from the roof.

The first step required all the pavers to be lifted. Initially, I could only move 3 pavers a day. At the end of the project I was able to move 8 pavers a day.

Where did God come into this? Paving was not something I was very experienced with and I tackled the task with little knowledge. I would get so far and then not know how to take the next step. Telling the Father that I would have to leave it to Him, I would leave the project on hold until an idea/ thought came on how to proceed, then I would check out how it fitted with the required next step. If it made sense and looked like working, I would implement that idea. Gradually the path was completed including reducing the height of one step and eliminating a couple of others. I was pretty pleased with the outcome. It looked good and provided a safe pathway.

AN EXAMPLE OF a big need was an occasion when I needed company and practical support at a very trying time. Bad weather several months earlier caused the postponement of a work task necessitating changes to the plans of other people. These weather caused changes resulted in the availability of the specific personal support I needed at that very trying and testing time. It was all in place before I knew I would need it and I didn't even have to ask for it. My deep need was met in an amazing way. What a wonderful Father!

I KNOW A lot of people find it hard seeing and accepting God as a Father because their own experience of 'father' has not been good. Despite our individual experiences, God is the Father we can get to know and rely on.

While I loved my Dad intensely he, like all of us, had struggles. I don't mean just financially but in standing up for me in a situation when I knew he wanted to but couldn't.

AT ABOUT THE age of ten, I had run away from home. I don't remember why but I must have been pretty upset over something and was doing a rebel thing with Mum. This big adventure of running away had me hiding in the corner of the grocery store we had next to my grandparents business. No risk of strangers or any other danger. My Dad found me and was relieved to have done so. However, what happened next was to me totally unexplainable. My grandmother 'lost it'. She was trying to whack my backside with a slat from the cod fish box while I was running around my Dad trying to avoid her. My Dad, dressed in his dark long coat just stood. It must have been a funny scene to anyone looking on but it tarnished my idea of a strong dad. Yet I knew he couldn't do anything because to do so would have made what I sensed to be a difficult situation even worse. In a way it showed lack of strength and courage and in another way it showed a strength. It was my pride that was being hurt more than my backside. I think if I had been in physical danger, he would not have hesitated to save me.

SOMETIMES CHILDREN CAN have a deep perception of what is going on even if they could not explain it. I have seen this within my own children.

WHY DO I feel confident in asking the Father for help with all my needs? Scripture! We find that right throughout both the Old and New Testaments there are many references to the stranger, the fatherless and the widow being cared for. The Church as a whole has not fully followed this instruction but I have found God is faithful.

CHURCh and school intertwined

THE CATHOLIC PRIMARY and high schools I attended were situated close to the church and the convent. School was an extension, not just physically, to the local Catholic Church and it was here we learnt our times tables and to write and memorise our catechism and prepare for the Sacraments of Penance, Holy Communion and Confirmation.

I WON'T SAY my school days were the best of times but it was certainly a time of learning: the three R's got prominence: reading, writing and 'rithmetic with the addition of social studies, Australian history with the adventures of the explorers, geography, a bit of Shakespeare, poetry, learning the Catechism and getting prepared for the Sacraments were all part of the school curriculum. An awareness of what was happening in the rest of the country provided a wider context for our lives. School and learning were where we started to find out where we fitted into the scheme of things though I don't know that I have really found that 'place of belonging'. I still feel that I am a pilgrim on a journey.

PRAYERS and Rituals

THERE WAS A variety of prayers and devotions we could say and do. These included the Mass, Rosary, Novenas, The Angelus and Benediction all of which I wholeheartedly took part in.

THE Mass

THE MASS WAS the pivot point of our church, school, family life and community. The Mass was something very special. It was a way of giving time to God. I loved the Latin Mass, particularly when it was sung in three part harmony with the pipe organ accompaniment. This gave a sense of worship with a language reserved for God. Yet, when I read the Bible, something didn't make sense. If Jesus died on the Cross 2,000 plus years back why are we still repeating this same sacrifice using symbols said to become His body?

THE Angelus

THESE WERE THE days when the church bell proudly rang to announce the time of the Angelus at 6am, 12 noon and 6pm. The bell was also rung to call people to Mass. I don't remember anyone at any time objecting to this practice. Even the townsfolk who weren't Catholic didn't object. The sound of the bell seemed to provide a continuity and connection and was a timepiece for everyone in hearing distance. The devout souls would stop and pray the Angelus in the workplaces, just quietly to themselves and no one took offence.

WHEN SCHOOL WAS in, the 12 noon Angelus was recited in each class room.
Generally the 'big' boys had the privilege of ringing the bell as its chain was rather heavy to pull. I considered it a treat when I got the rare opportunity to ring the bell usually during school holidays. Kids would think it fun to grab the bell chain and get a peal out in-between official times before running away.

APART FROM THE Angelus prayer time bell ringing out throughout the town on a daily basis (maybe we skipped the weekends) at Christmas another town wide Christian happening took place. This was the Salvation Army (the Salvos) Band travelling through town on the back of a truck playing Christmas Carols early on Christmas morning.
This was the beginning of Christmas Day!

NO ONE TOOK offence and it may have been 'safety' concerns which brought this practice to a stop.

THIS WAS A TIME when the wider community acknowledged God and there was acceptance of all who practised their Christian faith regardless of which part of the Christian church they were involved with.

ON SPECIFIC DAYS nominated by the Church, we young students would race to see how many indulgences we could get. There seemed to be no consideration for heart felt or sincere prayer and we probably were not even aware that the heart needed to be involved. The requirements for gaining an indulgence were: 'be in the state of grace' and the recitation of specific prayers. More about indulgences later.

DURING OUR RECESS or lunch break, we would run in and out of the church rattling off the required number of the Our Father, Hail Mary and Glory Be's getting through the required prayers as many times as we could fit in and by fulfilling the stated requirements fully anticipated getting some time off the expected purification time in Purgatory. We certainly wanted to avoid any and all pain. It seemed no one would be able to go to heaven without spending some time in this place that was a bit like hell but not as bad. One would eventually get out of Purgatory but once in hell, one was there forever.

More prayers and rituals will be covered as I journey on with my questioning.

WHAT is Purgatory?

DOES THIS TEACHING, which I have seen cause great distress to dying Catholics, have a basis in Scripture?

The way I understood this teaching was that even if we died 'in a state of grace' and would go to heaven, we had to first do time in Purgatory for purification so we would be holy enough to enter heaven.

I can imagine St Peter at the pearly gates checking our purifying time and sending us back to Purgatory if we hadn't been 'done' quite enough.

The scripture that is used as a basis for this teaching is from 1 Corinthians 3:15

Reading this passage in context from verse 10 we can reach a different understanding:

> According to the grace of God which is given unto me, as a wise masterbuilder, I have laid the foundation, and another buildeth thereon. But let every man take heed how he buildeth thereupon. For other foundation can no man lay than that is laid, which is Jesus Christ. Now if any man build upon this foundation gold, silver, precious stones, wood, hay, stubble; Every man's work shall be made manifest: for the day shall declare it, because it shall be revealed by fire; and the fire shall try every man's work of what sort it is. If any man's work abide which he hath built thereupon, he shall receive a reward.

If any man's work shall be burned, he shall suffer loss: but he himself shall be saved; yet so as by fire. (1 Corinthians 3:10-15)

These scripture verses are referring to man's work being destroyed by fire, not the man. Jesus did not die on the Cross to save works but to save man.

In Colossians Paul says:

Strengthened with all might, according to his glorious power, unto all patience and long suffering with joyfulness; Giving thanks unto the Father, which hath made us meet to be partakers of the inheritance of the saints in light: Who hath delivered us from the power of darkness, and hath translated us into the kingdom of his dear Son: In whom we have redemption through his blood, even the forgiveness of sins: (Colossians 1:11-14).

Even though 1 Peter is also used:

Wherein ye greatly rejoice, though now for a season, if need be, ye are in heaviness through manifold temptations: That the trial of your faith, being much more precious than of gold that perisheth, though it be tried with fire, might be found unto praise and honour and glory at the appearing of Jesus Christ: (1 Peter 1:6, 7) this Scripture does not justify the teaching of a place after death called Purgatory.

NOT ONE OF these verses provide a basis for the teaching about Purgatory. Pulling out individual verses to justify any teaching can lead to a grave misinterpretation of what was said and what was intended.

REGARDLESS OF HOW much time one might get to spend in Purgatory, the teaching that certain offences can be forgiven after death, is not backed by Scripture. Jesus told us in Matthew that blasphemy against the Holy Spirit would not be forgiven in this world nor in the one to come.

> *"All manner of sin and blasphemy shall be forgiven unto men: but the blasphemy against the Holy Ghost shall not be forgiven unto men. And whosoever speaketh a word against the Son of man, it shall be forgiven him: but whosoever speaketh against the Holy Ghost, it shall not be forgiven him, neither in this world, neither in the world to come. (Matthew 12:31-32)*

It is a bit of a stretch to understand from this Scripture that some sins will be forgiven after death when it is saying clearly that the offence of blasphemy against the Holy Spirit will not be forgiven now or in the future.

Death seems to be the point at which all choices are finished.

WHAT is blasphemy, this sin that will not be forgiven?

IN PRACTICE I understood that any talk or action against the church, the saints, the sacred things: medals, statues etc was blasphemy. Other things that were included in the catechism included slavery, torture or putting people to death. Over the years the church itself has not adhered to this. One has only to look at what happened to those who in the past disagreed with the teaching of the time or who worked to get the Bible into the hands of the ordinary person thus undermining the power of the priests and bishops. Not all misused their positions of power but enough did to cause pain.

Maybe the simplest and easiest understanding of 'blasphemy' is 'attributing to Satan something that God has done'.

MORTAL and venial sins

THEN WE HAVE the distinction between mortal and venial sins. Mortal sins were the 'biggies' and venial sins were the 'little ones'. Yet, all sin is an offence against God and it is not just the act of wrong doing or even not doing the action one should. Jesus took it much further when He said:

> *"Ye have heard that it was said by them of old time, Thou shalt not kill; and whosoever shall kill shall be in danger of the judgment: But I say unto you, That whosoever is angry with his brother without a cause shall be in danger of the judgment: and whosoever shall say to his brother, Raca, shall be in danger of the council: but whosoever shall say, Thou fool, shall be in danger of hell fire." (Matthew 5:21,22)*

Even our thoughts and words are enough to convict us.

A Story

WHEN MY HUSBAND died, several of my Mum's friends came to me and said 'He's not in Purgatory you know.'

I knew and believed this and was encouraged by what these ladies shared.

It was some time later that I prayed saying words like 'Father I believe that he is with you. I don't know how You can do it but is there some way You can show me if he is with You?'

Several weeks passed and then I had a dream. Now, I am not into dream interpretation and the way I would handle dreams, good or bad, which I woke up remembering was to pray 'Jesus, if there is something you want me to learn from this dream, would you please show me or take it from me.' When I had bad dreams where there was no lesson from God all memory of them disappeared. However, this dream was interesting and I still remember it.

The setting was a shop and I was with another person looking at fabrics. I looked over and could see my husband standing near a wall. What appeared to be hospital equipment was lying on the floor. My husband was not attached to this equipment.

I turned to the person I was with and said 'He is alive and well.'

In the dream I was aware I could not communicate with my husband and neither of us attempted to do so. It was not long after that I was reading in Genesis and the words 'alive and well' seemed highlighted. I was comforted and know I will meet up with him again.

R J Thesman says "We can't know everything that happens after death — and truthfully — we probably don't want to know everything. Yet I believe God is so loving, he sometimes allows us to "see" or "feel" into another realm to remind us he is omnipresent and always caring."[3]

YEARS AGO, I read an anonymous quote that still encourages me today: "Since God is with us, and our loved ones are with Him — then they're not very far away."

We know that the day will come when we will be raised with incorruptible bodies and that the dead will rise first.

What a day that will be!!!

WHAT are Indulgences?

WHILE I CAN find no Scriptural basis for the granting of Indulgences it seems they may have begun many centuries ago.

As I was taught, an indulgence gave one remission from the punishment due to us because of our sin even though we had been forgiven. Yes, we do have consequences to our actions both good and bad but an indulgence is a focus on punishment.

A consequence is related to the action but the punishment is a penalty imposed.

Our life experience has already shown us that we enjoy or suffer the consequences of our choices and actions in the here and now.

My understanding of scripture is that though we bear the consequences of our sin, which is hell and eternal death if we do not repent and accept God's forgiveness, that is not punishment for sin - it is a consequence of sin. An example of this is David in 2 Samuel 11.

DAVID WHO WASN'T out with his warring men as he should have been, saw a beautiful female neighbour, Bathsheba, washing and lusted for her. After sleeping with her, he arranged for her husband, Uriah, to come back to report on the progress of the fighting. David expected Uriah to take advantage of this opportunity to see his wife and then there would be no suspicion if a pregnancy resulted. Uriah was conscientious in his approach to his work responsibilities and had respect for his men who were still on the battlefield, so he didn't take advantage of this trip home to visit his wife even after David got him drunk. David then arranged for him to be in the thick of the fighting with the result he was killed. With adultery and murder on his conscience, he realised he had displeased God. In Psalm 51 he acknowledges his sin, asks for mercy and to be washed of his sin. Nathan, the prophet, tells David that his sin has been taken away and he will not die but God had judged and as a consequence of his sin, there would be violence in his house, his wives would be given to another and the child would die.

As Proverbs 10:16 and Paul in Romans 6:23 tell us, the wages of sin is death. The Good News of the Gospel is that Jesus paid for our sins through his death so we can have life. We can accept that gift or reject it.

INDULGENCES SEEM TO have originated within the Catholic Church but may have been copied from the Muslim practice of promising great rewards in the afterlife.

Raymond Ibrahim in his book 'The Sword and The Scimitar,' writes that in 1211 or so 'Pope Innocent II declared a crusade and ... the whole world should be absolved from their sins, and this pardon was [granted] because the king of Morocco said he would fight against those who adored the cross throughout the world.' Two centuries earlier Pope Urban 'had decreed that Christians fighting and dying against Muslims in Spain earned remission of sins'. Earlier still Popes Leo IV, Nicolos and John VIII 'also offered Christians who died fighting Muslims remission of sins.' Byzantine

Emperor Leo VI (d. 912) 'speaks with some respect of the doctrine of the [Islamic] holy war and of its military value, and even suggests that Christians might be well advised to adopting something of the kind.' 'Decades later Emperor Nikephoros Phokas tried "in vain to persuade the Byzantine church to adopt a doctrine similar to the Muslim doctrine of martyrdom", to no avail,' (Raymond Ibrahim (2018) pg 128)[4]

According to al-Tirmidhi, an Islamic scholar, in his book 'The Virtues of Jihad'[5] a martyr gains special favours from Allah including forgiveness of his sins, is wed to 72 beautiful maidens, is crowned and can intercede for 70 of his relatives.

The Crusaders, in their zeal to protect Christian pilgrims and recover the Holy Land from the Muslims, killed most of the non-Christians including horrific treatment of the Jews. The Jews tried to defend themselves but were burnt to death or sold into slavery.[6]

Somehow we are expected to believe that the committing of these atrocities could gain an indulgence giving one some remission of the punishment due for sin. Did the behaviour of some of the Crusaders, marching under the Cross of Christ, differ very much from the barbaric actions of those they were sent to attack and protect others from? Like all troops in battle, there are individuals and groups who take advantage of the situation to indulge their own brutality.

A BRIEF READING of history tells about the horrible atrocities carried out in the name of Christ and one is left wondering if this is part of the opening of the seals in Revelation 6 specifically in relation to the different coloured horses.

In recent times I have read that there are Bible scholars who have likened these horses to spirits seeking to control through religion, war, finance and disease with the white horse being the spirit counterfeiting the return of Jesus on a white horse in Revelation 19:11.

A discussion on this is beyond the scope of this writing but would be an interesting study to undertake.

PRAYING for the Dead[2]

WE SAID LOTS of prayers for the dead. Masses were offered for family members on the anniversaries of their deaths and we had a special annual celebration on All Souls Day.

I struggle to find more than one scripture that suggests praying for the dead is a good idea and that is where Judas Maccabeus made atonement for the dead, that they might be delivered from their sin and yet Peter, in 1 Corinthians 15, queried the value of people getting baptised for the dead. My short experience with bible study has shown that scripture will support not contradict another scripture and using one verse to base a belief on is far from adequate.

ON THE OTHER hand we find Job praying for his children while they were alive.

> And his sons went and feasted in their houses, every one his day; and sent and called for their three sisters to eat and to drink with them. And it was so, when the days of their feasting were gone about, that Job sent and sanctified them, and rose up early in the morning, and offered burnt offerings according to the number of them all: for Job said, It may be that my sons have sinned, and cursed God in their hearts. Thus did Job continually. (Job 1:4, 5)

Note that Job was praying for his children while they were still alive.

We pray for ourselves, our families and others here and now. We are not waiting to pray for people after they die. Using Job 1:5 as a basis for praying for the dead is a false understanding of what is written.

According to Paul writing to the Corinthians:

And as we have borne the image of the earthy, we shall also bear the image of the heavenly. Now this I say, brethren, that flesh and blood cannot inherit the kingdom of God; neither doth corruption inherit incorruption. Behold, I shew you a mystery; We shall not all sleep, but we shall all be changed, In a moment, in the twinkling of an eye, at the last trump: for the trumpet shall sound, and the dead shall be raised incorruptible, and we shall be changed. For this corruptible must put on incorruption, and this mortal must put on immortality. So when this corruptible shall have put on incorruption, and this mortal shall have put on immortality, then shall be brought to pass the saying that is written, Death is swallowed up in victory. O death, where is thy sting? O grave, where is thy victory? The sting of death is sin; and the strength of sin is the law. But thanks be to

God, which giveth us the victory through our
Lord Jesus Christ. (1 Corinthians 15: 49-57)

HOWEVER, GOD IS outside time and he sees the beginning from the end and everything in between. Could it be that what we are looking towards in the future has already taken place in the spiritual world???

WITHOUT STRETCHING THE meaning of scriptural passages there is no biblical basis for the doctrine of Purgatory, forgiveness of sin after death or praying for the dead. The one passage from Maccabees is not enough to hinge a doctrine on, it is also not good hermeneutics.

NOT only did we pray for the dead, we prayed to the dead

OVER THE HISTORY of the Catholic Church, many great men and women have been canonised - titled 'saints'.

Quite a number had special gifts and were prayed to for help in specific circumstances eg St Anthony of Padua was asked for help in finding lost items; St Jude was prayed to for help in helpless situations; St Christopher was always petitioned when travelling etc.

I had my favourite saints I prayed to for help until I started to realise that these men and women had died and were still dead. Jesus was the one who had not only died but had risen from the dead so why was I praying to dead people?

Why talk to the clerk no matter how smart or spiritual, when I could talk to the boss?

FIRST Confession and First Communion

WE WERE ALL around 7 years old and had already made our First Confession. How we practiced the words 'Bless me Father for I have sinned ...'

There was always some discussion about what type of sins we might have committed and I'm sure the parish priest of the day heard multiple repetitions of the same list: horrible to younger brothers and sisters; back answering parents; telling lies; disobedience. We reckoned it didn't really matter if we had sinned or not as long as we had something to confess. After Confessions were over and we were back in the playground there was the comparison of penance given - this was often 3 Hail Marys with an occasional Our Father or decade of the Rosary - with suitable banter re the severity or otherwise of the Penance given.

I RECALL A Confession time a few years later. It was a Saturday morning and I had been sent over to the church to go to Confession. Dutifully I did as I was told only to find the priest was away. Having been sent to go to Confession, obedience was called for. I confessed my sins to God and He forgave me my sins. To me there was nothing amazing about this. God listened to me and answered me.

A few weeks later, my mother asked if I had gone to Confession when she had sent me. My response was 'Yes'. This was the truth as far as I was concerned. However, I must have told a number of fibs as a child because my mother actually checked up and found out that the parish priest was away at that time so I was called to account. If I said I had talked to God and He had talked to me, I felt that wouldn't go down too well so I responded with 'There was a visiting priest.' This was also checked on and the result was a round of the strap for telling lies.

FIRST COMMUNION

I CAN REMEMBER my First Communion Day quite clearly, though I would have to look up the actual date. I was very excited about this day on which Jesus would come into my heart through Holy Communion. All us girls were wearing our very white dresses and veils. There was much 'oohing' and 'aahing' over each others dresses and making sure curls and bobby pins were in the right place. The boys were looking smart in their grey serge shorts, long socks, polished shoes and jackets. Despite joining in the social activity because I wanted to be part of the group, I was wanting to be alone to think about Jesus coming into my heart. This was a very special and precious time. I don't remember all the lyrics of the First Communion song we sang but it included these words

> *"I wish my little heart to be A cradle fair and gay Where Blessed Jesus may repose On my First Communion Day"*

I OFTEN WONDERED when did Jesus leave my heart so that I had to continue to receive Him in Holy Communion? I don't think I ever verbalised that question because ... well questions were not welcomed.

Asking "Why" questions such as 'why does the priest have to stand between me and God?' or "why do I have to confess my sins to a priest when I can talk to God?" weren't always treated with seriousness or that was my perception. 'Just believe what the Pope says' was a standard response.

When I say 'stand between me and God' I mean that the priest was seen as the go between. He was the one who heard our confession and gave absolution on behalf of God. He not only led the prayers, he said all the prayers and we only got to do the responses and Amens.

LOOKING BACK FROM the vantage point of more understanding of the Old and New Testaments and some history of the Jews and their relationship with God, I can see a resemblance to the Jewish rituals and priestly duties that were set out when God gave the commandments and instructions to Moses. This also carries through to the life and death of Jesus and the tearing of the veil to the Holy of Holies in the Jewish temple at the time of Jesus' death. With the curtain torn, everyone had access to the Holy of Holies. Jesus was both priest and sacrifice and we, the ordinary, the weak, the outcast could now all come to Him. No longer was a priest required to stand before God on our behalf. Jesus was the fulfilment of the law. Jesus himself said

> *Think not that I am come to destroy the law,*
> *or the prophets: I am not come to destroy,*
> *but to fulfil. (Matthew 5:17))*

CHURCH Service and Responsibility

AS I GOT older I was able to take on more responsibility in the Church. The Sanctuary and Sacristy became my special place to be. Here no one could tease or torment me. Here I was in charge answering only to the nuns or the Parish Priest.

I polished that brass til it shone and there were many brass candles and vases that needed attention. Dusting of all surfaces and washing and polishing the floor were diligently undertaken as this was the place Jesus lived. It was so very special to be able to look after God's place. The place where He lived was in the tabernacle before which a lamp was always burning. This was a bit confusing for a young child: Jesus lived in the Host in the Tabernacle and yet He came to live in my heart at Communion.

I HAVE SINCE come to realise that I am a tabernacle and that Jesus lives in me as He does in anyone and everyone who acknowledges their sin and accepts the sacrifice of the Cross that gives us eternal life.

And I heard a great voice out of heaven saying, Behold, the tabernacle of God is with men, and he will dwell with them, and they shall be his people, and God himself shall be with them, and be their God. (Revelation 21:3)

Together, individuals form the Body of Christ and His Body is the Church. It is not a particular religion or organisation. The Body Of Christ is more than this.

Now ye are the body of Christ, and members in particular. (1 Corinthians 12:27)

* * *

And let the peace of God rule in your hearts, to the which also ye are called in one body; and be ye thankful. (Colossians 3:15)

* * *

Whereby, when ye read, ye may understand my knowledge in the mystery of Christ) Which in other ages was not made known unto the sons of men, as it is now revealed unto his holy apostles and prophets by the Spirit; That the Gentiles should be fellow heirs, and of the same body, and partakers of his promise in Christ by the gospel: (Ephesians 3:4-6)

CHURCH helper duties

MY DUTIES AS a helper in the Sacristy extended to making sure there were enough Communion wafers in the Ciborium and wine and water in the cruets ready for Mass as well as laying out the vestments for the priest to put on. Every article had a meaning and was set out in a special way in the order in which they were put on. The following is as I remember:

First to be laid out was the CHASUBLE, which was not as voluminous or as light as more modern day ones. This was folded and placed so the priest could easily slip it over his head. This is symbolic of charity and also a tent or little house.

The CINCTURE was like a rope belt tied around the waist with a prayer for chastity.

The STOLE, representing the yoke of Christ, was tucked under the cincture.

Then the ALB, which is the long white robe worn as a symbol of the white robe of Baptism, was placed on top folded back in such a way that the priest could easily put it on.

The AMICE, the last item to be placed but the first item to be put on, is put on the head (symbolising the helmet of salvation) before being pulled back, the ties crossed over the chest going round the back and then tied at the waist in the front.

All of this symbolism and attached prayer was good and provided a meaning to the ritual but I was beginning to wonder if it was necessary. Any thoughts along this line were tucked back into place because this was the way of doing things and was by God's direction, therefore I couldn't wonder or disagree.

SACRIFICE - as in an altar sacrifice

IT WAS IN later years that I started to equate the Mass and vestments and their meanings with the ancient Jewish temple worship, their robes and their rules.

Was all this ritual of clothing and specific prayers really needed now?

When Jesus came to earth, didn't He fulfil the Law?

When Jesus died on the Cross wasn't He the ultimate sacrifice?

ON THE CROSS Jesus cried out 'It is finished' meaning that He had completed what He had set out to do and there was no longer any need for the animal sacrifices of the Old Covenant. These annual sacrifices were a forerunner to the sacrifice that God Himself would provide for the forgiveness of sins - His precious Son, Jesus. He was to be the ultimate sacrifice, a male lamb without blemish as a peace sacrifice offered at His own will to fulfil the requirement of the law for a blood sacrifice as the penalty for sin.

As the writer to the Hebrews wrote:

> *For such an high priest became us, who is holy, harmless, undefiled, separate from sinners, and made higher than the heavens; Who needeth not daily, as those high priests, to offer up sacrifice, first for his own sins, and then for the people's: for this he did*

once, when he offered up himself. (Hebrews 7:26,27)

Jesus obeyed the Father and freely gave up His life on the Cross. It is finished!

After this, Jesus knowing that all things were now accomplished, that the scripture might be fulfilled, saith, I thirst. Now there was set a vessel full of vinegar: and they filled a sponge with vinegar, and put it upon hyssop, and put it to his mouth. When Jesus therefore had received the vinegar, he said, It is finished: and he bowed his head, and gave up the ghost. (John 19:28-30)

Since the Crucifixion we can understand what the Psalmist David meant when he wrote:

Sacrifice and offering thou didst not desire; mine ears hast thou opened: burnt offering and sin offering hast thou not required (Psalm 40:6)

In Proverbs we are told:

To do justice and judgment is more acceptable to the LORD than sacrifice. (Proverbs: 21:3)

The Lord in speaking to the prophet Hosea said:

For I desired mercy, and not sacrifice; and the knowledge of God more than burnt offerings. (Hosea 6:6)

And in Matthew's gospel Jesus says:

"But go ye and learn what that meaneth, I will have mercy, and not sacrifice: for I am not come to call the righteous, but sinners to repentance." (Matthew 9:13)

Continuing on into the New Testament, the writer of Hebrews tells us:

For if we sin wilfully after that we have received the knowledge of the truth, there remaineth no more sacrifice for sins,. (Hebrews 10:26)

and that Jesus' sacrifice has put away sin:

For Christ is not entered into the holy places made with hands, which are the figures of the true; but into heaven itself, now to appear in the presence of God for us: Nor yet that he should offer himself often, as the high priest entereth into the holy place every year with blood of others; For then must he often have suffered since the foundation of the world: but now once in the end of the world hath he

*appeared to put away sin by the sacrifice of
himself. (Hebrews 9:24-26)*

As proof that there is no need for further ongoing
sacrifices, Jesus now sits at the right hand of God.

*But this man, after he had offered one
sacrifice for sins for ever, sat down on the
right hand of God; (Hebrews 10:12)*

Our sacrifice now should be as the Prophet Micah tells us:

*He hath shewed thee, O man, what is good;
and what doth the LORD require of thee, but
to do justly, and to love mercy, and to walk
humbly with thy God? (Micah 6:8)*

and in Hebrews:

*By him therefore let us offer the sacrifice of
praise to God continually, that is, the fruit of
our lips giving thanks to his name. (Hebrews
13:15)*

AS ALREADY MENTIONED, at the time of Jesus' death the
massive curtain in the temple that separated the Holy of
Holies, where only the High Priest could enter once a year,
ripped from top to bottom. We, the common people, now
had access to the Holy of Holies.

And, behold, the veil of the temple was rent in twain from the top to the bottom; and the earth did quake, and the rocks rent;. (Matthew 27:51)

and

And the veil of the temple was rent in twain from the top to the bottom. (Mark: 15:38)

Jesus was the High Priest who sacrificed, not animals, but Himself for the forgiveness of sins.

He paid the price.

No longer did animals have to be sacrificed as a symbol of forgiveness.

No longer were sacrifices required.

With the veil torn, our access to the Holy of Holies is through Jesus:

Jesus saith unto him, I am the way, the truth, and the life: no man cometh unto the Father, but by me. If ye had known me, ye should have known my Father also: and from henceforth ye know him, and have seen him. (John 14:6,7)

Jesus told the Samaritan woman at the well:

But the hour cometh, and now is, when the true worshippers shall worship the Father in spirit and in truth: for the Father seeketh such to worship him. God is a Spirit: and they that worship him must worship him in spirit and in truth. (John 4:23,24)

THROUGH GIVING IN to a desire to control or thinking we know better, have we made worship be something that was not intended after Jesus gave His life as a sacrifice to redeem us from the powers of Hell?

The New Testament confirms the Old Testament.

In Mark 7:7 Jesus told his disciples:

Well hath Esaias (Isaiah) prophesied of you hypocrites, as it is written, This people honoureth me with their lips, but their heart is far from me. Howbeit in vain do they worship me, teaching for doctrines the commandments of men. (Mark 7:6,7)

When one thinks back to when God told Abraham to sacrifice his son, Isaac, and as they journeyed to the place of sacrifice, Isaac had a question.

And Isaac spake unto Abraham his father, and said, My father: and he said, Here am I, my son. And he said, Behold the fire and the wood: but where is the lamb for a burnt offering?And Abraham said, My son, God will provide himself a lamb for a burnt offering: so they went both of them together. (Genesis 22.7, 8)

44

The ram caught in the thicket was God 's provision for Abraham's offering thereby saving Isaac for the continuation of God's plan for the salvation of mankind.

AS TIME WENT on, the Israelites were in bondage to the Egyptians and needed to be saved so that God's salvation plan could continue. At that point God instructed them on sacrificing or killing a lamb whose blood was to be applied to the door post so the angel of death would pass over. The story continues with the exodus from Egypt and all that followed. Years passed by until it was time for the plan for the salvation of all mankind to be implemented. God then provided the Lamb to save us from eternal death. This Lamb was His Son Jesus.

Jesus is worthy of our worship.
We worship Him alone.

THINKING OF WORSHIP led me to question if Mary and the saints are revered or worshipped in the Catholic Church. Praying to Mary and various saints was standard practice throughout my childhood. If one needed help in any way there was always a saint to meet the situation. Catholic church teaching is that the Blessed Virgin is honoured with special devotion which differs, though I sometimes wonder how, from the adoration that is given to Jesus.

Luke, in the first chapter of his Gospel, tells us about the Annunciation or the announcement by the angel Gabriel that Mary was to conceive, by the power of the Holy Spirit, a son and she was to call him Jesus. Mary exercised her free will to agree to what God asked of her. It was at the Council of Ephesus in 431 that the Church confesses that Mary is truly 'Mother of God,' yet nowhere in the Bible, which is acknowledged as 'spirit led', is there mention of Mary by this title.

Can an extrapolation based on human belief and understanding really be called a firm foundation for a belief?

And how does one differentiate between 'special devotion' and 'adoration' when, in the dictionary, similar words are used to describe both activities?

Is not praying to Mary, as in the Hail Mary, asking her to pray for us not in keeping with the idea of worship?

In China, the Chinese Communist Party (CCP) is not happy with people praying to God or acknowledging a higher power in any way. They want people to pray to Xi Jinping even to the extent of removing crosses etc and replacing them with pictures of Xi Jinping. They, the CCP, think and act on the understanding that praying to and before pictures is worship.

IT WOULD THEN stand to reason that if Jesus is God and worthy of our worship and somehow someone deemed Mary to be 'Mother of God', then she too should be worshipped, yet this is not what God has asked of us. It doesn't make sense unless one is needing to have a female equivalent to one of the pagan goddesses of ancient times who were worshipped as Queen of Heaven. To me there is too much of a mixture of human thinking and pagan worship thereby adding to the Word of God. This is something we are warned about in the Scriptures.

LET US CONSIDER what worship is.
According to the dictionary: 'worship' is the feeling or expression of reverence and adoration for a deity.
An action of worship can be bowing down (kneeling).

> *O come, let us worship and bow down:*
> *let us kneel before the LORD our maker.*
> *(Psalm 95:6)*

In the Old Testament there are many references to bowing down before people, other gods, carved images and engraved stones.
Daniel was one of the heroes of the Old Testament who would not bow to a statue. This landed him in the lion's den

as punishment by King Darius but God rescued him in an amazing way. It is an interesting and encouraging story. Grab a Bible and read Daniel 6. While you are there check out the story of Daniel's three mates, Shadrach, Meshach and Abednego and their experience in the furnace. (Daniel 3)

WHAT ARE WE DOING when we kneel before a statue?

Is not the bowing of the head, the knee or kneeling an act of worship?

Is not addressing the name of the statue, be it Mary, one of the saints or an angel when in a reverent posture a sign of worship?

AT THE RECENT Amazon Synod at the Vatican, a pagan idol was worshipped and yet what differed in that situation that upset so many people[11,] who would think nothing of kneeling, bowing and praying in front of a statue in the Church?

I FULLY AGREE with their outrage at the goings on in the Vatican garden but tell me what is the difference between one statue and the next?

It does seem a little contradictory especially to those looking on and who see no difference between one statue and the next.

WE NEED TO get this right because idolatry is something that God does not want His people to be involved in. He spoke and acted very strongly to the Israelites when they got involved with pagan worship and, in Revelation we are warned about a statue that we will be forced to worship. (Rev 13).

SOME YEARS BACK, God challenged me on this very issue but more about this later.

IS there a difference between worship and idolatry?

EVEN AN IMAGE that was used for healing in the Old Testament became an idol.

> *And the LORD said unto Moses, Make thee a fiery serpent, and set it upon a pole: and it shall come to pass, that every one that is bitten, when he looketh upon it, shall live. (Numbers 21:8)*

Later we read in 2 Kings 18:4 that Hezekiah, when he became king of Judah,

> *removed the high places, and brake the images, and cut down the groves, and brake in pieces the brasen serpent that Moses had made: for unto those days the children of Israel did burn incense to it: and he called it Nehushtan.(2 Kings 18:4)*

JUST AS IT was easy for the Israelites to take something God meant for good at a specific time and turn it into an item to be worshipped, so it is easy for the individual, regardless of official church teaching, to turn something into an idol.

WHEN SATAN WAS tempting Jesus in the desert he used these words:

And saith unto him, All these things will I give thee, if thou wilt fall down and worship me. Then saith Jesus unto him, Get thee hence, Satan: for it is written, Thou shalt worship the Lord thy God, and him only shalt thou serve. (Matthew 4:9,10)

We are told in Deuteronomy 4 that if the Israelites were to forget their Covenant with the Lord, He would scatter them to other lands and

> *there ye shall serve gods, the work of men's hands, wood and stone, which neither see, nor hear, nor eat, nor smell. (Deuteronomy 4:28)*

A QUESTION: Why would one worship something which cannot respond?

I CAN UNDERSTAND that as humans we look for something concrete on which to hang our faith but God through Scripture tells us this is the very thing we are not to do

> *Take heed unto yourselves, lest ye forget the covenant of the LORD your God, which he made with you, and make you a graven image, or the likeness of any thing, which the LORD thy God hath forbidden thee. For the LORD thy God is a consuming fire, even a jealous God. (Deuteronomy 4:23, 24)*

In the next chapter of Deuteronomy we read:

Thou shalt not bow down thyself unto them,
nor serve them: for I the LORD thy God am
a jealous God, ... (Deuteronomy 5:9)

Both Matthew and Mark record Jesus quoting from Isaiah:

This people draweth nigh unto me with their
mouth, and honoureth me with their lips; but
their heart is far from me. But in vain they
do worship me, teaching for doctrines the
commandments of men. (Matthew 15:8,9)

* * *

He answered and said unto them, Well hath
Esaias (Isaiah) prophesied of you hypocrites,
as it is written, This people honoureth me
with their lips, but their heart is far from
me. Howbeit in vain do they worship me,
teaching for doctrines the commandments
of men. (Mark 7:6,7)

Jesus said:

But the hour cometh, and now is, when the
true worshippers shall worship the Father
in spirit and in truth: for the Father seeketh

such to worship him. God is a Spirit: and they that worship him must worship him in spirit and in truth. (John 4:23, 24)

HOW do we worship the Father in the Spirit and in truth? In Chronicles 16:29 we are told to:

Give unto the LORD the glory due unto his name: bring an offering, and come before him: worship the LORD in the beauty of holiness. (1 Chronicles 16:29)

and the Psalmist tells us to:

O worship the LORD in the beauty of holiness: fear before him, all the earth. (Psalm 96:9)

Paul says in Romans:

I beseech you therefore, brethren, by the mercies of God, that ye present your bodies a living sacrifice, holy, acceptable unto God, which is your reasonable service. (Romans 12:1)

The writer of Hebrews goes into some detail about the first covenant worship and what is expected now. He lists various aspects of the temple, their arrangement and talks a little about the duties of the priests and the high priest in relation to the offering of blood for the sins of himself and the people. This sacrificial ritual had to be repeated because it could not do away with sin as it was comprised of things that were related to human activity. However, when

> *Christ being come an high priest of good things to come, by a greater and more perfect tabernacle, not made with hands, that is to say, not of this building; Neither by the blood of goats and calves, but by his own blood he entered in once into the holy place, having obtained eternal redemption for us. (Hebrews 9:11,12)*

In the next chapter the writer goes on to say that the law of the past was pointing to the reality of what was to come and there was no way the annual sacrifices would make people perfect. Therefore

> *when he (Jesus Christ) cometh into the world, he saith, Sacrifice and offering thou wouldest not, but a body hast thou prepared me:*
>
> *In burnt offerings and sacrifices for sin thou hast had no pleasure. Then said I, Lo, I come (in the volume of the book it is written of me,) to do thy will, O God. ... By the which will we are sanctified through the offering of the body of Jesus Christ once for all. (Hebrews 10:5-7,10)*

THE POPE, the successor to Peter[2]

ANOTHER THING THAT puzzled me for years was the claim by the Church that Peter was the successor to Jesus and was the first Pope and other Popes followed. To me the Scripture doesn't say this. I know I'm not a biblical scholar but God's Word is for all people and so should be able to be read and responded to by all.

From the Catholic Catechism we learn the Lord made Simon alone, whom he named Peter, the 'rock' of his Church. (881)[2] This statement could be justified by the Scripture verse that reads:

> *And I say also unto thee, That thou art Peter, and upon this rock I will build my church; and the gates of hell shall not prevail against it., (Matthew 16:18)*

However, is a Pope following on from Peter in church tradition what was really intended?

We know that 'Peter' means rock but is he the Rock on which the church is built or is it Peter's statement in verse 16 where Peter's answer to Jesus' question '*Who do you say I am?"*

> *And Simon Peter answered and said, Thou art the Christ, the Son of the living God. (Matthew 16:16)*

COULD IT BE that this statement is the Rock? The foundation of belief in Jesus who took on human flesh to fulfil the prophecies of salvation? The message of the Old Testament is one of God wanting His people to trust Him and not look to other gods. From the Old Testament we learn that Jesus is the Rock.

In The Song of Moses:

> *Because I will publish the name of the LORD: ascribe ye greatness unto our God. He is the Rock, his work is perfect: for all his ways are judgment: a God of truth and without iniquity, just and right is he. (Deuteronomy 32: 3,4)*

and

> *... then he forsook God which made him, and lightly esteemed the Rock of his salvation. (Deuteronomy 32:15)*

We could deviate here to discuss the topic of salvation and where salvation is found. Briefly, the above verse from Deuteronomy tells us that the Rock (namely Jesus) is the source of our salvation, not the church regardless of denomination. The church can lead to and assist in helping us find salvation but is not our salvation.

BACK TO THE ROCK ...

THERE ARE A couple of references to the Rock in this Song of Moses and a question regarding the whereabouts of the rock they would take refuge in instead of trusting in the One who created them.

We can move onto Samuel:

> *The God of Israel said, the Rock of Israel spake to me, He that ruleth over men must be just, ruling in the fear of God. (2 Samuel 23:3)*

and Psalms:

> *The LORD is my rock, and my fortress, and my deliverer; my God, my strength, in whom I will trust; my buckler, and the horn of my salvation, and my high tower.*
>
> *For who is God save the LORD? or who is a rock save our God?*
>
> *The LORD liveth; and blessed be my rock; and let the God of my salvation be exalted. (Psalm 18: 2, 31, 46)*

* * *

> *Unto thee will I cry, O LORD my rock; be not silent to me: lest, if thou be silent to me, I become like them that go down into the pit. (Psalm 28:1)*

* * *

Bow down thine ear to me; deliver me speedily: be thou my strong rock, for an house of defence to save me. For thou art my rock and my fortress; therefore for thy name's sake lead me, and guide me. (Psalm 31: 2,3)

* * *

He only is my rock and my salvation; he is my defence; I shall not be greatly moved
    He only is my rock and my salvation: he is my defence; I shall not be moved.
In God is my salvation and my glory: the rock of my strength, and my refuge, is in God. (Psalm 62:2,6, & 7)

IF THERE IS any argument that Jesus Himself is not the Rock and belief in Him is the not the Rock on which his church was built, we only have to look at what Paul writes in the New Testament:

As it is written, Behold, I lay in Sion a stumbling stone and rock of offence: and whosoever believeth on him shall not be ashamed. (Romans 9:33)

* * *

And did all drink the same spiritual drink:
for they drank of that spiritual Rock that
followed them: and that Rock was Christ. (1
Corinthians 10:4)

AT NO POINT did Peter proclaim himself as the rock on which the church was built. He regarded himself as an apostle and servant of Jesus Christ. See 1 and 2 Peter:

Peter, an apostle of Jesus Christ,

and

Simon Peter, a servant and an apostle of
Jesus Christ,

When Cornelius knelt to worship him, Peter would not allow it.

And as Peter was coming in, Cornelius met
him, and fell down at his feet, and worshipped
him. But Peter took him up, saying, Stand up;
I myself also am a man.(Acts 10:25,26)

IF PETER WAS the Rock on which the church was built and if he was the first Pope then, as history has shown, all the popes who have followed him certainly did not follow his example.

CONSIDER FOR A moment this question: 'How could the Church or Body of Christ be built on a flawed and sinful human?'

Yes, God has and does use each willing and available believer to help in building His church but the foundation is not built on any human except the One who became man to bring about our salvation.

SCRIPTURE CLEARLY SHOWS that Jesus is the Rock on which the church is built.

VATICAN II

VATICAN II WAS a major event during my early teen years. This huge happening had several effects on me and my life.

One was the change to what was classed as a 'Mortal' sin. I couldn't understand how, suddenly, at the stroke of a pen, the seriousness of a sin could be altered from a major sin deserving of hell fire if not confessed prior to death to a 'venial' or minor sin.

My teaching as a child had missing Sunday or Holy Day Mass or skipping various fasting occasions (without dispensation) as a mortal sin among other things such as murder. Changes were certainly needed but to a young person raised to believe in the Catholic Church and its laws as coming from God, the changes made by man undermined that sense of God given authority. This change by Vatican II caused me to question the Catholic Church even more.

How could such a drastic change be made?

How many people over the years suffered anxiety because they thought they had committed mortal sin?

I remember thinking that for years people had tried to live under the 'mortal' sin rule with many falling short and even maybe thinking they were headed for damnation and suddenly someone, a mere man, has decreed this is no longer so.

I was puzzled!

How could this be?

However, life moved on and because I could not see another way, I maintained our Catholic practice.

INTERESTINGLY, VATICAN II played a part in an aunty leaving the convent after 25 years. When I asked her some years later why she left, she said that after Vatican II, her vows no longer had any meaning. She didn't elaborate and the conversation moved on.

VATICAN II BROUGHT a number of other changes. The biggest was probably the change from Latin to one's local language for the Mass. Latin had always seemed to me to be God's language and when the Latin Mass was sung in three part harmony, with incense wafting through the church, one could feel as if one was in the throne room of God.

However, it did not take long to get into worship in the language we knew and spoke because that was how we were speaking to God in our own prayer anyway.

ANOTHER CHANGE WAS access to the Gospels apart from the readings at Mass.

I WAS ONE of many girls from throughout Australia who had been chosen by their schools or parishes to attend a school holiday training programme on how to conduct Gospel discussions. For the first time, as far as I was aware, we were able to read, study and talk about the Gospels without them just being read at Sunday Mass and, if the priest was able, an explanation of the Gospel coming through the homily.

It was wonderful to be able to talk about Jesus and what He said and did and to be able to encourage others to join in this conversation

VATICAN II MAY also have had some effect on the way even older people reacted to the Church and the Pope.

SOME YEARS AGO, my mother's group of friends (they all met at daily morning Mass when it was available) told me that they didn't follow the Pope because they felt that what the Pope said these days was not relevant to their lives. They told me that the connection they had with each other through the Church, the Mass and other Parish events was their community.

This sense of community or belonging is something I do miss but when brothers and sisters in Christ meet, there seems to be an instant connection that reaches across all divides of society.

Maybe this connection with God and each other is something the enemy, the satan, is wanting to break down and remove. Everything that God has deemed good, has been attacked. This includes marriage, our maleness and femaleness, pregnancy, birth, when and how we die, how we are governed and even how we are to think and speak - every aspect of the life God intended for us has been affected.

WHILE WE, THE Body of Christ, stay connected to the Head, the gates of hell will not prevail.

A Big Question

NOW THE BIG question for me was how do I recognise what are God's rules and laws and what are man's rules?

I always tried, though failed more often than not, to obey God's rules and I figured if God was unchanging, His rules had to be unchanging too.

So another step on my faith journey.

The Catholic Church was presented as being all knowing about what God wanted and the Pope was infallible in matters of doctrine so why did God change His mind on what was a major sin and what wasn't?

Something just didn't 'gel'.

With this question hovering in the background of my mind, I continued on being a full participant in the Church while following Paul's injunction to search the Scriptures.

> *These (the people from Berea) were more noble than those in Thessalonica, in that they received the word with all readiness of mind, and searched the scriptures daily, whether those things were so. (Acts 17:11)*

SCHOOL days are over - learning continues

AFTER FINISHING SCHOOL and working for a short time, I won a scholarship to undertake a Secretarial course in a bigger country town which necessitated leaving home and boarding. This move led to interesting times in learning to live with another family and eventually finding board of my own - still also sharing a room with another girl and subject to the rules of the house owner. I got into trouble a couple of times with staying out past our curfew or going to the drive in - both misdemeanours were threatened with a phone call to my parents. I never heard anymore so I assume those calls were no more than threats.

AS A TEENAGER away from home, the Young Christian Workers (YCW) provided the foundation for social involvement. With weekly 'Gospel Discussion' groups, monthly Sunday night dances and private activities such as tennis, water skiing, Friday night balls (in season), dances run by other church groups and the weekly Saturday night Town Hall Dance - our social life was packed with lots of fun, new activities and a growing understanding of where we fitted into the wider community.

As I was growing up I would say 'when I am 17 I am going to do everything I want to.' My dad would respond "young lady, when you are 17 you will do what you are told".

When I was 17 I did do everything I wanted to and 'had a ball' so much so that I didn't want to turn 18. My teenage years were fun.

On one occasion when back home for a weekend, I commented 'Dad, you don't know half of what goes on.' To which he replied 'Don't I? Your mother and I were young once.'

Thankfully no bad stuff happened and I did have a great time working, dancing, playing tennis, learning to drive (in a Holden), joining the rep theatre and enjoying all the great activities a big country town offered. On looking back I can see instances where things could have gone down a different track and I may have made different choices. However, I have felt that my Heavenly Father has had His protective hand on me throughout my life and, in retrospect, can see where He has helped me avoid the temptation to head in a not so good direction.

WEEKDAY Mass

WHILE LIVING AWAY from my family, I still found myself going to weekday Mass several mornings a week though the church was further away than I had been used to. Attending morning Mass involved a bit of an uphill trek but I loved those early mornings out. As a child, I had always preferred week day Mass to Sunday Mass because those who went during the week were there because they wanted to be there. The atmosphere was very different to Sunday Mass where many people went because they 'had to'. No one wanted to die in a state of mortal sin. The teaching at the time was that it was a mortal sin to miss Mass on Sundays and Holy Days of Obligation and it seemed this seriousness was also attached to the eating of meat on Fridays, Ash Wednesdays and every Friday during Lent. As discussed earlier, the rules regarding this were changed at Vatican II

THE CONTINUING DAILY sacrifice still didn't make sense.

Didn't Jesus die once and for all?

So why are we still carrying out a sacrifice, even a bloodless one?

To me, the Mass is similar to the Old Testament sacrifices, which were signs of what was to come, and in themselves, did not give salvation.

There are no instructions in the New Testament regarding repetition of the death of Jesus.

Paul tells us in his letter to the Romans that

For in that he died, he died unto sin once:
but in that he liveth, he liveth unto God.
(Romans 6:10)

Jesus died once on Calvary.

We remember His death and His giving up of life (His Body and Blood) taking on Himself the punishment for our sin, when we partake of the Bread and Wine.

Paul gave us clear directions on this in chapter 11 of his letter to the Corinthians.

Jesus didn't tell us to repeat His death but to remember it and what that sacrifice has done for us when we partake of the Bread and Wine. When I read the Catholic Catechism section on 'The Celebration of the Christian Mystery', it seems to me that we have taken what Jesus instructed and what Paul taught us, placed some complicated understanding on and rules around what occurred in early church days, and turned it into something more.

MARIAN devotion

DEVOTION TO MARY played a large part in my life.

As a child I ever so carefully and tenderly washed and dusted the statues and ensured no damage was done to them. Scapulars and medals got the same reverence. I didn't see myself as idolising these items but on looking up the meaning of the word 'idolising' when I sensed God was challenging me on this, I found it also means extreme admiration, love, or reverence for something or someone[6]. More of this later.

There was great emphasis on the Immaculate Conception of Mary and as a young child I was more than happy to go along with this concept. It did make sense that if Mary was the Mother of God, then she had to have been born free from original sin. It was this doctrine on the Immaculate Conception that would many years later lead to questioning even more my Catholic faith and my trust in the church and its teachings.

CHILDREN of Mary

DURING HIGH SCHOOL years I became a 'Child of Mary' wearing the medal of the Immaculate Conception on a blue ribbon, a white veil and blue cloak.

We were taught that because Mary was the Mother of God, she could not have had sin in her heart and the belief was that Mary was conceived without original sin unlike the rest of us.

The teaching on Mary as the Mother of God came from the Council of Ephesus in 431 which interestingly was called together by the political ruler Emperor Theodosius II, his co-emperor Valentinian III and with the agreement of Pope Celestine I.

The purity of Mary was said to be carried into her marriage to Joseph as she remained a virgin. This is an interesting interpretation of the Scripture as there are references to Jesus' brothers and sisters and Psalm 69 seems to describe Jesus' childhood and, if that is so, His childhood bears no resemblance to that perfect little family from Nazareth that had been so much a part of my childhood teaching and belief.

AFTER MARRIAGE WE were no longer called 'Children of Mary' nor could we wear the blue cloak and white veil. It seems our purity was tied into our sexual life more than our thinking and living. Purity means more than abstaining from sexual intercourse. Being a virgin and being pure are not synonymous.

When a Child of Mary married, she would wear her blue cloak over her wedding dress. Her fellow Children of Mary would greet her at the church doors and would remove her blue cloak. Did this mean that when I was married purity was no longer an issue? Considering 'pure' means (of a person) without malice, treachery, or evil intent; honest; sincere; guileless, it seemed to me that there was some discord with the thinking and teaching at that time. Maybe it had to do with the emphasis on celibacy and vocations.

THE Legion of Mary

I ALSO JOINED the Legion of Mary, a lay catholic organisation with the aim of giving glory to God through the holiness of its members by prayer and active cooperation in the work of Mary and the Church. There were weekly meetings with prayer and reports of work undertaken and other works allocated to be carried out weekly.

My work was most often hospital visitation. Our prayer was 'O Mary, conceived without sin, Pray for us who have recourse to thee.'

This is the doctrine of the Immaculate Conception and comes from the belief that because Mary is the Mother of God she could not have been born a sinner.

NOVENA to Our Lady of Perpetual Succour

OUR SATURDAY NIGHTS always seemed to start with meeting at the church for Saturday evening Novena to Our Lady of Perpetual Succour. It was here we decided on the activity for the rest of the evening. This may have been going to the pictures but more often than not, the local dance at the Town Hall won out. I remember the Town Hall Crawl - that dance movement one made when one had no clue as to how to dance but enabled movement around the dance floor.

WHAT is a Novena?

A NOVENA IS generally public or private prayers said on 9 consecutive days. A Novena to Our Lady of Perpetual

Succour (Help) was a public prayer practice held on a Saturday evening and consisted of Benediction (a specific Catholic service including the exposition of the Eucharistic Host in the monstrance and the blessing of the people) and prayers before an icon of Our Lady of Perpetual Succour. This picture, originating as an icon in the fifteenth century, is an image of Our Lady holding in her arms Jesus as a little King.

SATURDAY EVENING NOVENA was almost standard practice even after moving interstate, connecting with others through work and the YCW and eventually meeting my future husband to be.

Novena was generally the beginning of our Saturday night outings until we married, moved to a suburb further away and set up our first home.

PRAYER

ONE OF THE questions the School Inspector would ask was 'What is Prayer?' Answer: 'Prayer is the raising of the heart and mind to God'.

Prayer can take many forms. It can be joyful praise, desperate petition, deep gratitude, heart agony or daily conversation. It is an acknowledgement that we ARE by His grace.

PRAYER WAS PART of our dating and courtship and prayer continued into our married life. We nearly always prayed together before going to sleep. There were times, when I would be really cross and angry about something and in no mood for conversation or discussion, and my husband would just say 'Are you going to pray tonight?' This always took the wind out of my sails and, though the sun may have already gone down on my anger, the day generally (I can't say 'never') did not end up in anger.

I REMEMBER PRAYING late one night for one of the teenage children and in my mind thinking of the steps I could take to assist in the situation. I was taken aback when I heard from behind and above me 'Butt out!' I repeated the words, then heard 'Yes, butt out. I will deal with this.' So, I butted out and our Heavenly Father dealt so beautifully with the situation. I couldn't have pulled it off if I had tried

PRAYER GOT ME through many a night caring for a sick child; children's struggles and teenage tempests. I don't know how we would have survived through the ups and downs of life if we couldn't run to God with our troubles and triumphs. I know belief in God has been referred to as 'just a crutch' but a crutch is just what one needs when it is difficult to walk.

VOCATIONS

AT THIS TIME the big emphasis in the church was on vocations. We were encouraged to aspire to a Vocation. To be a priest was the ultimate! Families were very proud of having 'a priest in the family'. The girls could not be priests but we could aim for the lesser vocation of joining one of the many varieties of religious Orders for women. The boys, who didn't think they would make it to the priesthood, could take the second option of joining the Brothers of which, like the convents, there were a number of different Orders with a variety of emphases.

IT SEEMED TO be a higher calling to be a priest, or a brother, if male and a nun if a female. The celibate life seemed to be given a higher honour than the married life. Thinking on this causes one to wonder if this specific emphasis undoes the view of God that His creation of male and female was 'good' and His instruction that they go forth and multiply certainly doesn't pertain to a celibate life. Mmm! Has the Catholic Church had the wrong emphasis on God's creation all these years? Has making the 'single' life a life of full service to God not what God had intended for His creation?

> So God created man in his own image, in the image of God created he him; male and female created he them.

And God saw every thing that he had made, and, behold, it was very good. (Genesis 1:27 & 31)

However, in later years I question the concept of the single life in service being promoted as the best life to aim for. There are many people who, because of circumstances or life choice, live celibate lives and this does free them up to undertake ministries or work that a married person would find difficult. These people are to be encouraged, supported and included in the church community more so in this day when sexual activity is seen as the norm for all from puberty onwards and an accepted part of the dating scene though this is not what God intended. Celibacy is a gift to be honoured and not denigrated as it seems to be these days. Young people wanting to wait until marriage to enjoy the delights of sexual intercourse are treated as abnormal. They are not strange and need to be encouraged in this desire as it sets the foundation for trust in the marriage relationship.

MY Vocation

FOR A NUMBER of my fun teen years I often thought about entering the convent. A couple of times I made an attempt to talk to a priest about this vocation but these proposed meetings never took place. I was usually the one with the excuse. This was partly out of rebelling against the expectation of other people throughout my childhood that I would follow in my aunty's footsteps.

Eventually, I decided that I couldn't continue on this see saw of 'will I? or won't I'? So I sat down and wrote a letter of inquiry to the Sisters of Mercy and placed it in an envelope ready for posting. I went to bed, slept soundly, got up the next morning, picked up that letter, ripped it up and binned it. I knew that I knew that I knew that joining the convent was not to be. My mother commented later in the week about the convent and I told her that was one thing I was not going to do. 'So you are not waffling anymore!' was her response. The interesting thing is, I wasn't aware that my mother was aware of what was going on in me. Mothers do often know things about their children even if they haven't been spoken about. I don't know if my children have woken up to that yet.

MY VOCATION WAS to be the married life though I didn't know it at that time. I just knew I had made the right decision and even if I didn't have plans for the future it was OK.

I had a sense of 'something is going to happen' but I had no clue as to what. I felt at peace about my present and my future and that was just fine.

SOME MONTHS LATER I met my husband-to-be and had another of those 'I knew that I knew that I knew' moments that related to my future. It did take some time before we got to know each other enough to reach the point of the question being posed and a sparkling ring placed on a finger.

LIFE in the Church after Marriage

AFTER MARRYING AND setting up home in a totally new area for both of us, we looked forward to becoming a part of the parish, but this didn't work out as we expected. Both of us had been used to being fully involved in the Church and related activities in our parishes and now we were trying to find our place in a new situation where we were the 'newbies' and didn't quite 'belong'. I taught some Scripture classes in the local high school and a couple of times played the organ/piano at church and yet, even after being in this parish for about 4 years and getting 2 babies baptised, there was still not a sense of belonging.

I could not pinpoint why we both felt this.

IT WAS IN the mid 70s when we moved interstate for work reasons and finally purchased a home and settled down with a growing family. Our involvement in our local parish was much smoother this time. Partly because the community in this area was mainly transient and strangers were more readily accepted. Another reason too was that we had become involved in the community through preschool and kindergarten. Having children opens up many doors.

Family

DURING THIS TIME, my 6th pregnancy commenced. I had miscarried three times previously as well as giving birth to two boys. Now, I was having bleeding issues again. A friend collected the two boys and cared for them while I had some in bed rest, which helped and the pregnancy proceeded. It wasn't easy going as I was also coping with a prolapsed uterus. This had been diagnosed prior to heading interstate and corrective surgery wasn't an option because I couldn't or wouldn't say that we were not having anymore children. As the specialist explained, if I fell pregnant (what a terrible term 'fall pregnant'), after this surgery, all the corrective work would be undone.

INTERESTINGLY AT THIS time, my mother was involved with the Catholic Charismatic movement and had been telling me about God who answered prayer. This was a new approach to me. I had always had a relationship with God but to think that He would actually answer prayer to a physical need was a huge step in my thinking about who God was and what He did.

I HAD BEEN staying with my parents while doing some work for my old workplace and finding that if I had a day on my feet or just sitting all day at work the result would be feeling that everything, baby and all, was dropping out. To say I was uncomfortable was an understatement. So, on going to bed one night, I decided to take Mum at her word about God answering prayers and I prayed along the lines of 'Father you have given me this baby to carry and these two boys to raise and I can't do both so you will have to do something about it.'

DID HE?

YES, HE DID!

Amazingly and miraculously!

The next morning my 'bundle' was sitting higher and, apart from normal pregnancy discomfort, I experienced no further extreme discomfort and pain for the rest of that pregnancy or the following 5 pregnancies which went full term with healthy babies. At my post natal check after the birth of that first precious daughter, everything was back in place where it should have been.

I CAN'T SAY I was always thrilled with this healing.

I do remember, after having a pregnancy confirmed chasing my husband around the house with a broom while telling (or maybe yelling at) him that it was all his fault. His normal quick repartee stopped me in my tracks.

Despite his charm and diplomacy, I wasn't ready for another pregnancy and having to cope with an amazing amount of judgement from others about breeding like a rabbit.

I just wanted to crawl in a hole and hide for 9 months.

However, life goes on and somehow strength comes to deal with all that family living involves.

MIRACLES continue to happen

OUT WALKING WITH the baby in the stroller with the two older boys, one doing the right thing holding onto the stroller, the other very active one running up to the next corner and then running back to the stroller. I don't know where this child got his energy. He continued this activity until called back to stay with us as we had to cross a busy road.

He came running back and immediately headed down a steep driveway to a busy road. At the same time a milk truck, which had been parked to the right of the driveway, started moving. In my mind's eye I could see this two year old plastered into the side of the milk truck. There seemed to be no way he could stop.

The imagined impact did not take place.

I could not work out what had happened.

With thumping heart, I collected one young boy and imposing stern instructions to remain attached to the stroller, with threat of severe punishment if not obeyed, continued homewards.

What had happened?

I puzzled over this as we continued on our way home. I couldn't work out what had just happened.

When running downhill, it is difficult to stop one's momentum and come to a standstill.

This child had not stopped.

He actually came backward up the driveway.

The only way I could explain this was it was like someone had grabbed him by the back of his collar and pulled him back. An angel?

HOUSING experiences with a growing family

OUR GROWING FAMILY meant we were outgrowing our home. This led to selling up and renting for a time while building a house.

The decision to sell came at a down turn in the housing market and the agent did not want to put the house on the market at the price we said we wanted. She said it wouldn't sell. We asked for it to be marketed at our price for three months and, if it hadn't sold at that point, we would re-evaluate the asking price.

Within two (2) weeks the house had been sold at our asking price!!

WE FOUND A house that we were able to rent very cheaply. There was a lot of clean up work required before it could be occupied and it was our willingness to do this clean up that offset the rental. Financially we were in a good spot as we set about building a new family home.

Our eldest, though he helped us with the cleaning, didn't think much of living in this house. When told to hop in the bath at the end of our first day in this house, he stated that he wasn't having a bath in 'that bathroom' and that he wasn't having a bath til we moved into our new house. When told it would be at least six months before that would happen, he responded 'Oh! I thought it was going to be six weeks.'

However, the bathing did get attended to and we settled in or so we thought.

AFTER A TIME one of our sons began having nightmares where he was seeing frightening men. These were more than nightmares. He was seeing and describing a person even after waking and coming into our room. We could see nothing but this child was able to describe what he was seeing in detail and, at times, would be frigid with fear. We did everything we knew to deal with this: praying the Rosary; sprinkling holy water all round the house particularly all entrances - windows, doors. This didn't make any difference.

The night time visitors and scariness continued.

The situation came to a head one day when I went into town to meet the owner of the house to pay the rent. We had met with him several times in the course of arranging the rental but on this day, as this man walked towards me across the foyer, it seemed his eyes had changed and he was looking, not just at me, but through me in the most uncanny and scary way. Was there a connection? I did not know. I had not experienced anything like this before and I was quite unsettled.

Finally I decided I could no longer stay in the house with the children as sleep and health were being affected.

It was quite some years later before I learnt how to deal with these demonic annoyances.

We were able to find another rental quite close to where we were building and quickly moved in. This meant a big increase in rent and somehow we managed but a big plus was we were able to join the parish we were going to be living in when the house was complete.

A New Parish

WE NOW HAD the opportunity to settle into a new suburb and Catholic parish. The suburb had only been established for a few years and the infrastructure was still underway. Masses were held in the Catholic school hall until the church was eventually built and the parish continued to flourish.

MY HUSBAND WAS a shift worker, which was a disruptive lifestyle, so our social life revolved around family, work, school and the church. It was a busy but good time of life with ongoing learning in the area of belief and spirituality.

FOR A PERIOD of time after the birth of our sixth child we attended church in another parish (which came about when a part of our suburb was split from a large parish to form part of another parish). Here there was a sense of 'community' we hadn't experienced before. It was also a time of much learning as many shared more of their spiritual journey in conversation than we had previously experienced, and people tended to interact after Mass over coffee and even discussed the sermon. It was like the Mass didn't finish as soon as we walked out the door. This was so different to people exiting church and emptying the car park in very quick time.

BEING A NEW parish there was a school and no church. The Parish Priest held weekday Mass in his home and over time made a tiny prayer room on the front porch. This prayer room was available all the time.

ONE HAD AN increasing sense of what 'community' was all about - sharing faith and sharing life. In time this particular Parish Priest was moved on and, many of those who had formed this community drifted off. A few stayed in this parish, others went back to their own parishes and others went to other denominations. What stood out to me was that community had been formed more around the priest than around Jesus and it is Jesus who wants to be the centre of our lives.

AROUND THIS TIME the Family Group movement was adopted in many parishes. The purpose of this was to build up community and it achieved this quite well as small groups of people met for a social get-together on a monthly basis and an annual weekend getaway. As friendships developed there were more after Mass conversations with a wider range of people.

THERE WERE MANY activities or groups one could join. The Catholic Church provides many opportunities for day or weekends to focus on spiritual matters for those who can take part.

One such weekend was a turning point on another matter of belief - Limbo.

AT A PARISH Weekend, I was talking to several ladies and commented that I had lost three babies (miscarriages). The Parish Priest who was walking past overheard my comment, stopped and said 'They are not lost. They are with Jesus'. This thought blew my mind. I had been taught and understood that babies who were not baptised were in a place called Limbo.

What an amazing thought to think that these precious little ones were not lost. They were in the best place they could ever be: with Jesus.

I can't help but wonder how many mothers and fathers over the years have had heart ache because the little ones they had conceived and who miscarried, were stillbirths or died before Baptism could be undertaken, were considered to be lost to life with God.

It was only in 2007 that Pope Benedict XVI quashed the teaching of this tradition of unbaptised babies going to Limbo.[7]

Another 'tradition' or 'church teaching' that was incorrect and caused pain.

IN THE WEEKS following this Parish Weekend, I contemplated this new concept and in prayer asked God to give me names for these babies which I thought were girls. Why girls? I had told the obstetrician at the time of the miscarriages that I felt they were all girls to which he replied that some women could only carry one sex. Looking back, this made sense to me as I had carried and birthed 6 boys without problems but had issues with carrying and birthing both girls.

God honours heart prayer and His answer to this was 'Sarah, Rebecca and Rachel'.

A Story

SOME YEARS LATER I was looking after an aunt who was living in hostel type accommodation for the aged. She had reached a point where she was in need of more care than the facility could provide yet it was considered unwise to move her to their nursing home.

She had reached the point of not been able to feed herself and with the help of others we took turns to visit at a meal time and assist. This didn't last long as food was not of interest and she was spending most of her time in bed which meant I was having to get a private nurse in to care for her. She was very fearful as well as been uncooperative with the staff and becoming more uncommunicative.

I was visiting one evening and praying. 'Father, if there is something I can say that will take away this fear, will you please give me the words?'

As I sat with her, I thought about her childhood and the fact that we had both attended the same school and church a generation apart. I realised that we would have received the same teaching about Jesus dying on the Cross for our sins. I sensed to say to her: 'Remember that Jesus has forgiven you all your sins.' I didn't know if she had heard me so I repeated those words and she indicated that she had heard.

Shortly after this I had a discussion with a nurse about her personal care and the indication of a bed sore developing and what to do to make her more comfortable. It was decided to put an eggshell mattress on the bed.

I told her that we were going to put another mattress on the bed. She patted the mattress saying 'this is a good one.' I replied 'yes, but we need to do this to help stop your bottom from getting sore.' She said something I did quite catch and I asked her to repeat. She said 'I'm getting a new one.' It took me a moment to get what she meant. 'Oh,' I said, 'You're getting a new body?' 'Yes' she replied. Those were our last words to each other.

I visited the next evening and did not even feel the need to pray. I just read a book as I sat with her. She was not talking. She was no longer fearful.

The following morning, an hour before the private nurse was to commence her shift, I received a call saying that my aunt had just passed away peacefully and that in those last couple of days she had become cooperative and thankful for every thing that was done.

Prayer is not always answered as we would like or expect from our human view point as we can only see a very small part of the picture. But, prayer does get heard and does get answered.

There are many answers to prayer and as a verse from the hymn 'The Love of God'[8] says:

> Could we with ink the ocean fill, And were the
> skies of parchment made; Were every stalk on
> earth a quill, And every man a scribe by trade;
> To write the love of God above Would drain
> the ocean dry; Nor could the scroll contain
> the whole, Though stretched from sky to sky.

LIFE Continued and then came
a light bulb moment

WE WERE IN the process of building our own house which wasn't very far from where we were renting.

During the night of the 17th December 1979, 8 months pregnant and finding sleep difficult on a very hot night, I was walking round the courtyard saying the Rosary and asking Mary to help me through this time as she knew what it was like to be pregnant. As I contemplated Mary, her life as we knew it and how she was held up as the person to model our lives on, I realised that something was not quite right with this thinking.

If Mary was conceived without original sin and in a state of grace as the doctrine of the Immaculate Conception taught, then how could Mary's life be the model for my life?

If Mary was conceived without the sin that taints all of us, Mary had a head start and therefore really didn't know what I was going through. She was either a woman just like me but picked out and chosen by God to carry and bring Jesus into this world, or, the Catholic Church teaching on the Immaculate Conception was not correct. This teaching was only defined in 1854 by Pope Pius IX. Similarly, the belief in the Assumption of Mary was formalised even later in 1950. Neither of these beliefs has a basis in Scripture that I can find and, if Scripture is the Word of God, then these dogmas have been added and while beautiful concepts, believing them is not a requirement by God for salvation and life eternal.

Adding / Subtracting

THERE ARE A number of instructions in Scripture that warn about 'adding' to His Word:

> *Ye shall not add unto the word which I command you, neither shall ye diminish ought from it, that ye may keep the commandments of the LORD your God which I command you. (Deuteronomy 4:2)*

* * *

> *What thing soever I command you, observe to do it: thou shalt not add thereto, nor diminish from it. (Deuteronomy 12:32)*

* * *

> *Every word of God is pure: he is a shield unto them that put their trust in him. Add thou not unto his words, lest he reprove thee, and thou be found a liar. (Proverbs 30:5,6)*

* * *

> *For I testify unto every man that heareth the words of the prophecy of this book, If any man shall add unto these things, God shall add unto him the plagues that are written in*

this book: And if any man shall take away
from the words of the book of this prophecy,
God shall take away his part out of the book
of life, and out of the holy city, and from
the things which are written in this book.
(Revelation 22:18,19)

MARY

YES, MARY WAS a virgin and was the Mother of Jesus. There are many prophecies pointing to the Virgin Birth and we know Jesus's arrival fulfilled many prophecies. But Mary couldn't be the Mother of God as I had been taught. The church teaching itself was to me contradictory. On one hand the church taught that God is the beginning and end of all things and that He is above all creatures. On the other hand it teaches that Mary is the Mother of God.

What should one believe or maybe it was my understanding or misunderstanding of the teaching? Several times over the years in my discussions with other people I had been told 'you learnt your lessons too well.' I'm really at a loss as to how that works but I was taught that God always was and is and ever will be. If that is so, how can it be that Mary is His mother? She does not have the same credentials and, so, is not qualified for this role.

FROM THAT POINT on, I could not pray the Hail Mary because praying to Mary was like praying to another woman who, though greatly blessed, was just a woman. She was not God and therefore not a person I could pray to. The Magnificat, which we prayed often and the beginning of which forms the first part of the Hail Mary, suddenly made sense because previously, I could not understand why Mary referred to her spirit finding joy 'in God, who is my Saviour' if she didn't need a saviour. The Magnificat is a beautiful prayer of praise and a statement of the blessedness of Mary and her life AND how she too was in need of a Saviour. This prayer of praise can be found in Luke 1:46-55

IN MORE RECENT years I've come to see that Mary can be held up as a model, not just for me but for all of us. She faced many situations in her life which we don't really think about.

According to Dr William Welty who wrote about Mary[9] based on what is in the Scriptures, there were several 'tests', which Dr Welty poses as questions, that Mary faced and reading about how Mary addressed and moved through her 'tests' can be and is great encouragement to each one of us, both male and female.

These are some of the tests or questions posed:

Are you willing to trust God with your life?

Are you willing to give God your expectations about your life?

Will you remember who Jesus really is?

Will you give your dreams about your child to God?

The answers based on Mary's response, shows that Mary can be an example we can aim to emulate without attributing titles or beliefs over and above the facts.

FATIMA Apparitions

AS A CHILD I had a deep devotion to Our Lady of Fatima. I had a little cream coloured statue which I more than venerated along with other statues and items. More about this later.

I loved the story of the apparitions and all that went with them but I remember, even as a child, wondering why God would have the children do something as dangerous as walking backward on a rocky path. This didn't make sense to me as a child and I couldn't articulate what concerned me.

With some life experience behind me I came to realise that God does not place us in dangerous situations but at times, through our choices, allows them so we can know His protection and His grace.

On recently rereading The True Story of Fatima[10] I read so many things that don't fit with Scripture and further increases my thinking on 'how much more have I and others been misled?' and 'what is the real story behind the Fatima apparitions?' It is strange that the children looked for ways to do penance for sinners as requested by the lady but in doing so they deceived their own parents and possibly did their own health harm by not eating their lunch and going without water especially on hot days.

This extra stuff is so sad particularly when the core teaching of the Catholic Church is Jesus.

I was taught that believing in Jesus as the Son of God sent to pay the price for my sin is what is needed for my salvation.

Why add to this simple yet profound statement?

The Apostles' Creed is an all encompassing statement of belief in Jesus and all that He did as well as our response. This says it all.

> *I believe in God, the Father Almighty, Creator of heaven and earth, and in Jesus Christ, His only Son, our Lord, who was conceived by the Holy Spirit, born of the Virgin Mary, suffered under Pontius Pilate, was crucified, died and was buried; He descended into hell; on the third day He rose again from the dead; He ascended into heaven, and is seated at the right hand of God the Father Almighty; from there He will come to judge the living and the dead. I believe in the Holy Spirit, the holy catholic Church, the communion of Saints, the forgiveness of sins, the resurrection of the body, and life everlasting. Amen*

THE Rosary

THE ROSARY WAS an encouraged and favourite way of praying and consisted of saying an Our Father followed by ten Hail Marys and a Glory Be. This was repeated ten times while meditating on the Mysteries of the Rosary. These covered aspects of the life and beliefs about Mary and the life, suffering, death and resurrection of Jesus. To meditate on Jesus and His great love for us and talk to Him about it is a beautiful thing to do.

SAYING THE ROSARY as a family on a daily basis was to be encouraged. Mum insisted on this every night with the injunction that the family that prays together stays together. I don't know what other members of our family gained from this ritual but I do remember nudges, giggles and other childhood distractions. In later years I began to wonder how could one give heart and soul and mind to prayer if the spoken words differ to the thoughts of the mind? Where is the congruency in this type of prayer?

THERE WAS COMFORT in praying the rosary and even touching the rosary beads carried in one's pocket and then the question:

Was there any difference in this to playing with worry beads to calm the mind?

Is it a case of looking to something man made for help instead of to God our Creator?

Could this be the type of prayer Jesus was referring to when he told us:

> *But when ye pray, use not vain repetitions, as the heathen do: for they think that they shall be heard for their much speaking. (Matthew 6:7)*

TRADITIONAL stories

AS CHILDREN WE were taught about the 'little family of Nazareth' comprising of Jesus, Mary and Joseph and that Mary remained a virgin. This I was happy to believe and treasure. That was until I saw reference to Jesus' brothers and sisters in one of the Gospels. When I asked about this, I was told that they were members of Jesus' church family. After I had read the book of Psalms several times and I noticed that Psalm 69 indicated that the childhood of Jesus was not necessarily a happy one. Mary did consummate her marriage to Joseph. Jesus did have step-brothers and step-sisters, some of whom teased and tormented him as did the men who sat at the city gates, making up 'ditties' about his illegitimacy.

> *Because for thy sake I have borne reproach; shame hath covered my face. I am become a stranger unto my brethren, and an alien unto my mother's children. For the zeal of thine house hath eaten me up; and the reproaches of them that reproached thee are fallen upon me. When I wept, and chastened my soul with fasting, that was to my reproach. I made sackcloth also my garment; and I became a proverb to them. They that sit in the gate speak against me; and I was the song of the drunkards. (Psalm 69: 7-12)*

A number of David's psalms were prophetic and referred to the coming Messiah, Jesus.

If the stories I was told as a child were not true, but just based on an idealised tradition, then what other things had the Church taught that were not quite correct or not based on the Word of God, the Scriptures?

Was this story of the little Nazareth family similar to telling children about the fantasy of Santa or the Tooth Fairy because the truth was too hard or would undermine some commonly held beliefs?

JESUS HIMSELF SPOKE against the reliance on tradition.

If we read Jesus' words in the gospel of Mark. Chapter 7:8,9, we get an understanding of His position on tradition.

> *For laying aside the commandment of God, ye hold the tradition of men, as the washing of pots and cups: and many other such like things ye do. And he said unto them, Full well ye reject the commandment of God, that ye may keep your own tradition. (Mark 7:8,9)*

In Galatians Paul commented about being more zealous for his Jewish traditions. He did not seem to hold this up as a good thing.

> *And profited in the Jews' religion above many my equals in mine own nation, being more exceedingly zealous of the traditions of my fathers. But when it pleased God, who*

separated me from my mother's womb, and
called me by his grace, To reveal his Son
in me, that I might preach him among the
heathen;... (Galatians 1:14-16)

Paul in writing to the Thessalonians said,

Therefore, brethren, stand fast, and hold the
traditions which ye have been taught, whether
by word, or our epistle. (2Thessalonians 2:15)

In this Paul was not referring to future teachings by or traditions of the Catholic Church or any other group. At that point Paul only knew the Jewish scripture in which he was highly educated and in his zealousness for what he believed, he had been getting rid of the 'Jesus' rabble. THEN came his Damascus experience with Jesus.

When Paul spoke about traditions he was referring to what he and they already knew and held to be true. Paul would not have been thinking of what might come in the future. In fact, Peter gives a warning in Acts:

For I know this, that after my departing
shall grievous wolves enter in among you,
not sparing the flock. Also of your own selves
shall men arise, speaking perverse things,
to draw away disciples after them. (Acts:
20:29,30)

This is similar to the warning of Jesus in Matthew:

Beware of false prophets, which come to you in sheep's clothing, but inwardly they are ravening wolves. (Matthew 7:15)

We would do well to ask 'Who are these among us who are wolves in sheep's clothing?'

Over the centuries there are a number throughout many of the Christian churches who would fit this description.

And so continued the questioning journey that had begun as a child.

GROWING family

OUR FOURTH SON arrived at 6 am just as the rising sun was beginning to shine through the bedroom window.

This birth was a planned home birth for no specific reason than that it was to be that way.

Within half an hour after his birth, his brothers and sister were sitting on the bed delighting in this new addition to our family. His grandparents and aunties who were staying with us, were able to join in this delight. Having my mum on hand at this time was a wonderful blessing. One of the things she did that helped was bringing me hot wet cloths for my tummy to ease the after birth pangs. Hot wet cloths worked so much better than just heat packs. More fiddly and time consuming, but more effective and after many years, I still find this method effective to ease pain.

LIFE Changes

OUR LIFE HAD really changed by this point. Along with a new baby, our household increased in size with an extra two adults and two teenagers who had come to live with us while we built our new home with added accommodation for them.

Involvement in Church, school and other community activities continued.

TWO years on and another pregnancy

HOWEVER, I FELT that this baby was not going to make full term. We had undertaken a trip for me to attend a Women's Aglow conference. My husband and children were staying with relatives. The night before the conference I was telling my husband how I was feeling and that I needed to go to the doctor when we got home because I felt the baby had died. This was because the way I was feeling was just the same as when one of my earlier pregnancies had come to an untimely end. I attended the conference on day one and on day two was feeling quite 'off' and told a couple of the other attendees. Immediately, I was surrounded by women praying for me and my baby. My sense of well being improved and a check up on returning home indicated the baby was all ok and the pregnancy proceeded. Apart from a hiccup partway through, with contractions brought on by a period of extreme coughing, the pregnancy proceeded well, and on being told that I had given birth to a daughter, my immediate response was to say quite loudly: 'I'm the King's daughter!'

This was a wonderful answer to a deep deep heart desire. I loved my boys (and still do) yet deep down I was longing for another daughter.

OTHER God Moments

ONE EASTER STAYS in my mind.

On Holy Thursday after the beautiful ceremonies replete with flowers, candles, incense and singing, I was at Adoration of the Blessed Sacrament thinking on the suffering and crucifixion of Jesus and feeling a sadness at what had happened when I heard God, as an audible voice outside of me, ask 'Why are you sad?' My response was 'because Jesus had suffered and died for me.' God told me that this was a happy time for me because it was as a result of that suffering that I had eternal life.

I now appreciate the Cross in a different way - with a sense of sadness that it was my sins that put Him there and a deep sense of joy in His love for me and you that held Him to the Cross til He cried 'It is finished'.

FORGIVENESS of Sins

DURING THE FOLLOWING years I thought on and off about the Church's teaching that only the priest could forgive sins. This teaching puzzled me as it seemed to forget or ignore our personal responsibility to forgive others.

We met with a number of people for weekly bible study at the home of friends. This particular night we were discussing forgiveness and I commented that we all had the power to forgive sin as in the prayer Jesus taught his disciples and a prayer we continue to pray more than 2,000 years later - *And forgive us our debts, as we forgive our debtors ...*

Jesus went on to say:

> *For if ye forgive men their trespasses, your heavenly Father will also forgive you: But if ye forgive not men their trespasses, neither will your Father forgive your trespasses. (Matthew 6:14,15)*

Nothing could be said more clearly but raising this caused an upset. I was very loudly and very plainly told that only the priest could forgive sins. This discussion brought an end to that particular group. Concerned at having brought this time of bible study to an end, I went to talk to the Parish Priest and explained what I had said. He didn't seem to think I had spoken incorrectly, even though the Catholic Church teaching, as we understood it at the time, was that only in the Sacrament of Penance or Reconciliation through the priest that God grants pardon for sin.

THE FORGIVENESS PART of The Lord's Prayer where Jesus is telling us to ask for forgiveness based on our willingness to forgive others who commit offences against us, is consistent with the parable Jesus told in Matthew's Gospel about the servant and forgiveness or lack there of. When people sin against us, we are to forgive 'seventy times seven' which was Jesus' answer to Peter followed by the parable: about the king whose servant owed him a huge debt and who was facing being sold along with his wife and children in order to repay that debt. The servant asked for time to pay and promised to do so. He was granted this time. Later on the king got a report that this servant had tossed a debtor of his into gaol. So he called him and said:

> *O thou wicked servant, I forgave thee all that debt, because thou desiredst me: Shouldest not thou also have had compassion on thy fellowservant, even as I had pity on thee? And his lord was wroth, and delivered him to the tormentors, till he should pay all that was due unto him. So likewise shall my heavenly Father do also unto you, if ye from your hearts forgive not every one his brother their trespasses.(Matthew 18:32-35)*

Prior to this parable, Jesus also said to his disciples (and to us who follow):

*Verily I say unto you, Whatsoever ye shall
bind on earth shall be bound in heaven: and
whatsoever ye shall loose on earth shall be
loosed in heaven. (Matthew 18:18)*

At no point in Jesus' discussions with his disciples did he tell them they had to go to the Rabbi, or any other leader, to deal with sin. I can see the Catholic Church connection with the Apostles and those in authority who followed but that does not provide a basis for the priest being the only one who can forgive sin or who can 'bind and loose'.

WHEN WE STATE 'I can never forgive ....' we are binding ourselves to the other in an act of unforgiveness which is harmful to both parties. 'Unforgiveness' was once described to me as 'a dark cloud over you and the person you are unwilling to forgive and keeps you both connected even if you can't see it'.

It is generally known that many people are in hospital because of psychosomatic or 'soul' sickness. If we are in Christ, each of us has the responsibility and power, through Him because of His death and resurrection, to keep short accounts with each other.

My journey continued and in expressing my view or understanding of the workings of God put me in a spot or two but I didn't feel I could pretend to believe something just because I was told this is what I was to believe.

ONGOING Parish and School Involvement

THE PARISH AND school had grown quite large since its establishment and a nun (religious sister) was appointed to assist with parish work. Sister's view of the working and blessing of the Holy Spirit was consensus. This didn't make sense to me, so I put in writing my concern about seeing consensus in decision making as being a sign of the Holy Spirit at work. To my simple way of thinking, I had figured that if the people, involved in whatever the matter was under discussion, were in tune with the Holy Spirit, then there would be unanimous decisions, not consensus. I said that I thought Satan could use consensus for his purposes.

It was my mention of 'Satan' that seemed to cause a response to this communication, leading to being advised to make an appointment with and speak to the head of the Jesuits - nothing like going to the top!

I duly made the appointment with this priest and took with me a copy of my letter which he read. We chatted for a while and all he said was that Satan was stopping a lot of good being done because I was hesitant. Interesting! But, at the time, not very helpful and this did nothing to change my thinking on the way I thought the Holy Spirit would work, keeping in mind that the Holy Spirit is sovereign and can work in which ever way He chooses.

AFTER A TIME I did come to realise and understand the 'hesitancy'.

It was this: when an idea to visit someone, give flowers or bless another in some way, I would start to think about what I would gain from doing this 'good deed' and was only doing this 'good deed' for what I could get out of it. This thinking led to not following through with that action, thus good did not get done.

On thinking about this for a while and realising what I was doing or not doing, I changed tactics. When an idea to give a blessing was undermined by the thought of what I might or could get by doing so, I would go back to what my initial motive was.

What was I thinking about when that idea first came to mind?

If that thought was for the other and not myself, I knew I could follow through.

At times it wasn't easy to ditch my long term 'stinking thinking'.

SCHOOL Board

AT ONE POINT, I nominated for a position on the school board, which provided an opportunity for parents to become involved in and contribute to the spiritual and educational welfare of the students. I received a phone call asking me to withdraw my nomination, as it was thought this position would not be suitable for me or my abilities or some such reason. I hadn't really given much thought to what my abilities were or how to use them, and so figured someone else knew better, so I withdrew my nomination.

Maybe the questions I asked had something to do with it. Though I didn't like confrontation, I would take up an issue with a teacher or principal or whoever the appropriate person was.

As I thought about this further, I realised that this was a form of shutting someone up who may have held views that were contrary to the status quo.

I experienced this in a more direct way when I was dipping my toes into the waters of the political ocean. A newspaper can control what and who the public gets to hear about and so control the social agenda and even the outcome of elections.

As the years have rolled on this form of control has been taken to a whole new level through political correctness, shutting down debate and censoring market place discussion with moves to push this attack on free speech even into the home.

It is wise to be aware of the source of your news and social information and not take as gospel all that is presented on television, in newspapers or on social media.

CHILDREN'S First Sacraments Preparation

AS OUR CHILDREN moved through their school grades they were given the opportunities to make their First Confession and First Communion followed a few years later with Confirmation.

After the older ones had completed their preparation and received these early Sacraments, changes were brought in about how the children were prepared. The school used to carry the full responsibility for this preparation but now the parents were to be included in the preparation process. This was a good move towards more parental involvement in our children's education and we were happy to go along with these changes.

One year the parents were being encouraged to teach their children about the Father Heart of God. I wondered how we could be expected to do this when many parents didn't have this understanding or experience themselves. This was an aspect of God that we had not been taught about. Those who did have an understanding had come to that through their own personal experience of God.

AFTER ATTENDING ONE of the First Communion preparation meetings for parents, I got into a discussion with the school Principal regarding the psychologists' thinking that a person couldn't have a personal relationship with God til they were in their mid twenties. I disagreed with this. As far as I was concerned, I had had a personal relationship with God since about age 7 or 8. The Principal told me that I must be special, but I knew whatever I had was also available to everyone, and I really wasn't that special. What is wrong with people in places of influence that they can't see this?

MINISTRY Training or lack of

DURING THESE YEARS my husband and I found we were often approached by couples having marital issues and, while we could and did listen, we felt our conversations with couples or individuals seemed to go round in circles.

We had no training for this, so we went to chat with the Parish Priest asking how we could get training in this area. A pat on the back and 'you're doing a great job. Keep doing what you are doing' was all we got. This was far from satisfactory. We could see we needed to know how to ask questions to help get off the conversational merry go round and guide, through questions, the individuals to see solutions for themselves.

Eventually I was in a position where I could study and gained a Certificate IV in Christian Counselling.

IDOLATRY

I DON'T REMEMBER the timing but over a period of months I felt a conviction about how I 'cared' for, used and even prayed to my little statues, medals, rosary beads, scapulars (both brown and green) and a number of pictures that we had hanging on our walls.

Bowing before statues, kissing scapulars and medals was not reverence as I had been taught but, in God's eyes, was idolatry. This realisation came as a shock and was an agonising period. I so wanted to obey God, and here I was sensing that He was telling me to dispose of all my statues, medals, etc, and yet, this would be a sacrilegious act and blasphemy. I argued with God over this for a number of months. These items were precious, they were part of my childhood and growing up; they were part of my faith journey - I couldn't part with them let alone destroy them.

My husband couldn't see why I was getting so upset about this. He couldn't see any harm in these items, and a couple of them were wedding presents. However, I knew deep within my heart that I had idolised these things through bowing, praying and kissing and my Heavenly Father didn't want this to continue. He didn't want anything between Him and me. In scripture it does say that He is a jealous God.

For thou shalt worship no other god: for the LORD, whose name is Jealous, is a jealous God: (Exodus 34:14)

There are many more scriptures regarding idolatry.

I sought counsel and after hours of discussion, I left with these words ringing in my ears: 'You know in your heart what you need to do. Only you can make that choice.'

More weeks went by. I was at a point of decision! I could move forward or turn back.

I knew I could not turn back.

Interestingly, it was only recently that one of our adult children told me that as a child he couldn't understand why we were making them go to a church with idols. He added 'didn't God tell us not to have idols?'

As a child he had more understanding of what God asked of us than I did and we had not talked about it.

Now I can't help but wonder how far did I lead my children astray?

WHEN YOU THINK about it, what is the difference between bowing one's head and kneeling before a statue, be it Mary, Joseph or one of the many other saints, and what took part in the Vatican garden at the beginning of the Amazon Synod (2020)[11] with Pachamama?

[The Pachamama is a fertility goddess from Inca mythology and is revered by the indigenous peoples of the Andes where she is known as the earth mother.][12]

To stand before, bow before, kneel before a statue in prayer is worship and, as mentioned earlier, references in Scripture to worship included 'bowing'.

Ye shall make you no idols nor graven image, neither rear you up a standing iage, neither shall ye set up any image of stone in your land, to bow down unto it: for I am the LORD your God. (Leviticus 26:1)

* * *

For it is written, As I live, saith the Lord, every knee shall bow to me, and every tongue shall confess to God. So then every one of us shall give account of himself to God. (Romans 14:11,12)

* * *

O come, let us worship and bow down: let us kneel before the LORD our maker.(Psalm 95:6)

* * *

Wherefore God also hath highly exalted him, and given him a name which is above every name: That at the name of Jesus every knee should bow, of things in heaven, and things in earth, and things under the earth; And that every tongue should confess that Jesus Christ is Lord, to the glory of God the Father. (Philppians 2:9-11)

ACTION Taken

WE WERE HEADING off for the Christmas break and I chose this time to do or die.

I really thought that I would be struck dead when I destroyed these items but I knew it had to be done. On the other hand, maybe I was wanting to hold onto the innocence of childhood learning. When sharing this with a Catholic friend, she said that I had learnt my lessons too well and thought that kneeling, bowing or praying before statues was not an issue.

What did I do?

I gathered up all the items that I had given more than reverence to and placed them into a metal garbage can and set fire to them. After all had burnt and the fire was out (in Australia one doesn't leave a fire unattended) we set off on our trip.

Amazingly, nothing happened.

We enjoyed our travel and Christmas celebration and returned home. There was no repercussion and time went on.

Came March the following year and suddenly I realised I had an amazing sense of freedom.

Where did this come from?

The only thing I could put it down to was no more ties to caring for and, dare I say it, worshipping the little statues, medals, etc etc. Fear was gone!

It wasn't until many years after I realised that I hadn't given a thought to what my children would do without a mother if being struck dead was the outcome which, at the time, I thought could be a possibility.

PARENTAL Responsibility

WE WANTED TO be good parents and this involved teaching the children about God and the Catholic Church as well as the usual parental duties of caring, training, feeding, clothing, educating etc, but we found we were struggling to teach our children about God. Sundays and church involvement were more battle than worship. Getting seven children ready for Mass on Sundays was a challenge in itself and, added to that, was the objection by the children to going to Mass. We tried and tried and couldn't solve this and it didn't help to be told that we were 'building treasure in heaven'.

Where was the treasure in arguing etc etc.?

Were we not to be a light in a dark world?

We were not setting a good example for the benefit of church attendance.

Eventually a day came when my husband and I looked at each other and acknowledged that our first task as parents was to teach our children about God and we were not doing too good of a job of it. We could also see that the church was not helping.

What were we to do?

This led to us doing what was at one stage totally foreign and unthinkable - we started going to other churches and checking them out. This led nowhere so we let things stand as they were for a time.

TIME Moved On

MY HUSBAND BECAME involved with the Police Christian Fellowship and it was through the wife of one of the members that I began going to a Know Your Bible (KYB) study group through the church they were attending. I quite enjoyed these bible studies and the company of the women who seemed down to earth while being fully aware of Jesus working in and through their lives. They were 'living' their faith. Nothing in the studies contradicted anything I had come to understand and believe and I suggested that maybe this was a church we could visit and taste.

FOR A PERIOD of time we went to our local Catholic parish Mass on a Sunday morning and to the Sunday evening service at this other church. Going to a Sunday evening service was strange to us but it seemed many Protestant churches had both Sunday morning and evening services.

Came the end of January and this church was beginning the new year Sunday School programme.

Sunday school was another different concept for us. The closest we had come was the children being taken out of Mass for the first part of the Mass, including the sermon, and then coming back in for the Offertory, Consecration and Communion.

We discussed the situation and my husband said to put the children into Sunday School. We explained to them what we were doing and told the eldest that he didn't have to go every week but we did expect him to go to church with us as a family once a month. This was a big thing for him as he had flatly refused to go to Mass for quite some time. He agreed to this.

The first Sunday morning we attended church, I saw our son shaking hands with another young man and realised it was a school friend. He became involved with church life and went on to study and obtain a Diploma in Theology. While he was studying, I completed a Certificate IV in Christian Counselling and later on his youngest sister obtained a Batchelor of Theology. But, I digress.

THE YOUNGER ONES took to Sunday School and instead of the normal Sunday fights and arguments about church going, they were up and dressed ready to go. The usual bickering in the car on the way to church was replaced by conversation about what they were learning in Sunday School. This was more like it - children who were learning about God and His ways and how it applied to normal living. We now had a basis for discussing God things and learning and growing with the children.

They may or may not be walking with the Lord at this point in their lives but I know that they have a foundation. I know Jesus knows their hearts and where they are in their journey to and with Him and I believe He won't let them slip from his fingers.

> *And this is the Father's will which hath sent*
> *me, that of all which he hath given me I should*
> *lose nothing, but should raise it up again at*
> *the last day. And this is the will of him that*

sent me, that every one which seeth the Son, and believeth on him, may have everlasting life: and I will raise him up at the last day. (John 6:39,40)

* * *

That the saying might be fulfilled, which he spake, Of them which thou gavest me have I lost none.(John 18.9)

* * *

OUR Parish Situation

BECAUSE WE HAD been so much a part of the local Catholic parish and school, to go to another church was a huge step and was going to be noticed even if others had not been aware of our questioning.

I went to see the Parish Priest and told him what we were doing and why. I could see he was hurt but he didn't lecture us or try to change our minds. He seemed to understand our position, accepted us where we were at and just asked us to come to Mass occasionally so he knew we were still around. As the children were attending the local Catholic school, we frequently saw this Parish Priest.

My mother was also hurt by our decision to attend another church but became more accepting after I explained to her that she had taught me about God and that at this point, we felt this is was God was asking us to do. Other extended family members commented that we were losing our faith. Oh! if only we could explain that we were finding the only One in whom to have faith.

BAPTISM

AFTER A GAP of about 6 years, another baby was on the way and we were blessed with another little boy. I often said this was a child who shouldn't know how to hate because he was surround by so much love.

Came time for the baby to be baptised. Baby baptism wasn't a part of the church we were attending. Instead, they baptised adults (often down at the river) and new babies were dedicated to the Lord during the Sunday morning service.

I rather liked this but all our other children had been baptised in the Catholic Church so we wanted to continue this. My husband asked the Parish Priest if we could have the baby baptised and he agreed acknowledging that Sunday morning would not suit us. At this parish, Baptism's were conducted during or immediately after Sunday Mass. We asked if we could have the Baptism on the Saturday afternoon and he agreed.

As I was rushing around getting ready to head to the church, I suddenly remembered that a part of the Baptismal ceremony included a question about bringing the child up in the Catholic Church. I thought, 'Oh, I don't know how I can answer that. Well, Lord, you will have to deal with that for me.' and thought no more about it.

The Baptism ceremony went smoothly and afterward a friend came to me saying 'Father didn't ask you that question.' I asked 'What question?' She replied, 'the one about bringing up the child in the Catholic church.' I had not spoken to anyone about this and her awareness of it surprised me. This left me with gratitude for the Parish Priest who was looking to keep us connected and not chase us away as has happened with others - that is their story to tell.

THE Biggest Challenge - Communion

YES, DECIDING TO move from the Catholic Church was not an easy move despite all the questioning and soul searching that had gone on for years. The biggest challenge was Communion, which had always been a very special time for me going back to the day of my First Communion. Along with the beautiful memories of time with my Lord and Saviour was also the continuing question from that First Communion time: 'If Jesus comes into my heart in Communion, when does He leave so I have to receive Him again?'

I knew that sin drove Him out but what if I didn't sin?

I UNDERSTAND THIS mystery better now that I have learnt more about the Passover though it still remains a mystery as to why the God of the entire universe should send His Son Jesus to die as a ransom for us. Each of us could ask 'Why me?'

Paul, in his letter to the Corinthians, explains better what occurred at the Last Supper, which itself was a remembrance of the night the angel of death had instructions to pass over the Israelite houses which had blood of the lamb on the doorposts. The Blood of Jesus (indicated by the wine) is our protection from death. Jesus is the Bread of Life providing nourishment. In partaking of the Bread and Wine we are remembering this amazing provision of life now and into eternity.

For I have received of the Lord that which also I delivered unto you, That the Lord Jesus the same night in which he was betrayed took bread: And when he had given thanks, he brake it, and said, Take, eat: this is my body, which is broken for you: this do in remembrance of me. After the same manner also he took the cup, when he had supped, saying, This cup is the new testament in my blood: this do ye, as oft as ye drink it, in remembrance of me. For as often as ye eat this bread, and drink this cup, ye do shew the Lord's death till he come. (1 Corinthians 11:23-26)

MY CONCERN REGARDING Communion was put to rest when on reading about men in a concentration camp during the war years gathering together for Communion on Christmas Day. They were from different countries and different Christian denominations YET through that Communion Service (there was no priest), they felt connected to each other and their families who would also be receiving Communion that day. This connection through Jesus went beyond formal liturgy, beyond denominational boundaries, beyond circumstances, beyond time zones, beyond geographical distances.

For where two or three are gathered together in my name, there am I in the midst of them. (Matthew 18:20)

Jesus is the connection when we gather in His Name.

Have you ever felt that connection when you meet another who is a believer in Christ?

I WONDER IF there will come a time when Catholics will realise that Holy Communion, as currently and historically taken, is not quite what Jesus intended and Protestants will find that the Bread and Wine are really much more than they have thought and practised.

Maybe a better understanding of Jesus instructions to partake of the bread and wine can be found in understanding the Jewish Passover feast in conjunction with the celebrations of Holy Week. This I am yet to study.

MY QUESTIONING OF our tradition does not mean I am saying that what we have been doing is wrong. I am proposing that tradition may have held us back from plumbing the depth of the meaning of the life and death of Jesus.

Despite questions, the bottom line is:

> *Neither is there salvation in any other: for there is none other name under heaven given among men, whereby we must be saved. (Acts 4:12)*

JEWISH connection

WE CAN'T GET away from the fact that Christianity had its genesis in the Jewish Torah.

WHAT WAS EXPECTED by the Jews when they read in their Scriptures that the Messiah would come?
Paul tells us in his letter to the Corinthians:

> *Jews demand signs and Greeks look for wisdom, but we preach Christ crucified: a stumbling block to Jews and foolishness to Gentiles, (1Corinthians 1:22, 23)*

Jesus was not what the Jews were expecting. They were expecting a military person to deliver them from the hands of the Romans. To the knowledgable Greeks who liked to reason things out, the idea of Jesus, His Work and His Resurrection did not fit their expectations either.

WHAT DO WE understand from those same Scriptures that Jesus explained to the disciples on the road to Emmaus and the letters written after the Holy Spirit came at Pentecost?
Can we have full understanding now?
Paul said

> *For now we see through a glass, darkly; but then face to face: now I know in part; but then shall I know even as also I am known. (1Corinthians 13:12)*

THE empty Grave

THE RESURRECTION OF Jesus proves the Cross and gives us hope.

If the grave is not empty where is our hope?

And yet, we tend to give little emphasis to this amazing display of His power. People from a variety of professions have examined the Shroud of Turin and commented about the amazing power that was in the tomb that day.

Death, which is a consequence of sin, was proven to be dealt with by the Resurrection We no longer have to fear death.

> *O death, where is thy sting? O grave, where is thy victory? (1 Cor 15:55)*

THE RESURRECTION ALSO shows that Jesus has power over sin and all the sadness and sorrow it brings. This freedom from death and sin is available to all. Many refuse it but, His heart is that all would be saved.

> *For this is good and acceptable in the sight of God our Saviour; Who will have all men to be saved, and to come unto the knowledge of the truth. For there is one God, and one mediator between God and men, the man Christ Jesus; Who gave himself a ransom for all, to be testified in due time. (1 Timothy 2:3-6)*

WE PLACE A lot of emphasis on the Cross and rightly so. Without the Cross there is no redemption.

Maybe our understanding of the Cross and the spilt Blood on Calvary would increase if we took more time to reflect on the Resurrection of Jesus. and the giving to us of the Holy Spirit.

EVEN JESUS HIMSELF, in telling the story about the rich man in Hades and the poor man in heaven, acknowledged that knowing about His Resurrection would not be enough to persuade some people.

> *And he said unto him, If they hear not Moses and the prophets, neither will they be persuaded, though one rose from the dead.*
> *(Luke 16:31)*

Jesus showed Himself to the Apostles and other disciples after His resurrection in a number of situations.

Thomas didn't believe the others when they told him that Jesus was alive. His words reflect our doubting and yet Jesus' words to Thomas encourage us.

Thomas had said that he wouldn't believe unless he saw the wounds and put his hands into the wounds of Jesus.

> *After eight days the disciples, including Thomas, were gathered.*
> *Then came Jesus, the doors being shut, and stood in the midst, and said, Peace be unto you. Then saith he to Thomas, Reach*

hither thy finger, and behold my hands; and
reach hither thy hand, and thrust it into my
side: and be not faithless, but believing. And
Thomas answered and said unto him, My
Lord and my God. Jesus saith unto him,
Thomas, because thou hast seen me, thou
hast believed: blessed are they that have not
seen, and yet have believed. (John 20: 26-29)

ONE OF MY favourite parts of Scripture is found in Luke 24 when the women went to the tomb, found it empty, and the angels reminded them that Jesus had told them before he died that he would rise from the dead. After this two of the disciples headed to Emmaus. They were downhearted because the one they believed to be their Messiah and who was to save them had been crucified and to top it all off, the women couldn't find his body.

As the disciples walked along Jesus joined them but they didn't recognise him. He asked why they were so sad and after expressing surprise that he didn't know, they explained the recent happenings in Jerusalem to him.

Then he said unto them, O fools, and slow
of heart to believe all that the prophets have
spoken: Ought not Christ to have suffered
these things, and to enter into his glory? And
beginning at Moses and all the prophets, he
expounded unto them in all the scriptures the
things concerning himself. (Luke 25-27)

The day was drawing to an end so they invited Jesus to join them for the night. As they ate:

> *he took bread, and blessed it, and brake, and gave to them. And their eyes were opened, and they knew him; and he vanished out of their sight. And they said one to another, Did not our heart burn within us, while he talked with us by the way, and while he opened to us the scriptures? And they rose up the same hour, and returned to Jerusalem, and found the eleven gathered together, and them that were with them, Saying, The Lord is risen indeed, and hath appeared to Simon. And they told what things were done in the way, and how he was known of them in breaking of bread. (Luke 24: 30-35)*

HOW AMAZING TO have Jesus Himself explain the Scriptures?

Yet what Scriptures was He explaining to them? The New Testament was currently being lived and hadn't yet been written. The only Scripture they had and knew was what we call the Old Testament.

Was Jesus' explanation to these disciples about the law of the Old Testament and how the Messianic prophecies were fulfilled in him?

What was it about the breaking of the bread that caused them to recognise him?

Is it possible this some how ties into the Passover celebration from ancient times that they would have known and the Last Supper?

There is still so much to learn.

SCRIPTURE Teaching

OVER MY YEARS OF church involvement, there has not been a great deal of explanation of the Scriptures which hold so much history (His Story) and continuing revelation. Learning and understanding of the Scriptures has mainly been through small groups meeting on a regular basis to undertake 'Gospel Discussions' or 'Bible Study'. Listening to various Bible scholars has also proved enlightening. These can be, have been and continue to be exciting times of learning more about Jesus and the plan of redemption that was put in place in the very beginning:

> *And the LORD God said unto the serpent,*
> *Because thou hast done this, thou art cursed*
> *above all cattle, and above every beast of*
> *the field; upon thy belly shalt thou go, and*
> *dust shalt thou eat all the days of thy life:*
> *And I will put enmity between thee and the*
> *woman, and between thy seed and her seed;*
> *it shall bruise thy head, and thou shalt bruise*
> *his heel. (Genesis 3:14,15)*

Jesus is that offspring and through His death He struck the head of Satan. Through His Resurrection He gave us proof that He had won the victory over sin and death and we too can share in eternal life with Him when we believe in Jesus.

That if thou shalt confess with thy mouth the Lord Jesus, and shalt believe in thine heart that God hath raised him from the dead, thou shalt be saved. (Romans 10:9)

* * *

But these are written, that ye might believe that Jesus is the Christ, the Son of God; and that believing ye might have life through his name. (John 20:31)

* * *

Even the righteousness of God which is by faith of Jesus Christ unto all and upon all them that believe: for there is no difference: For all have sinned, and come short of the glory of God; (Romans 3:22)

* * *

But these are written, that ye might believe that Jesus is the Christ, the Son of God; and that believing ye might have life through his name. (John 20:31)

* * *

And this is his commandment, That we should believe on the name of his Son Jesus Christ, and love one another, as he gave us commandment. (1John 3:23)

WE DO NOt have to do anything for salvation. Jesus has done it all. The good deeds that we do, or the fruit we bear, comes out of our belief in Jesus as the Son of God and our desire to love and obey Him.

IT is now nearing the end of 2020 ...

... AND WHAT a challenging year this one has been. In spite of all that is going on around the country and the world, our life journeys move onward and together our faith can grow as we learn, experience and share more about the plan and ways of God.

Reading the Bible continues to open up more of God's plan for humankind now and in the future. Have you ever pondered on the future when Jesus will be ruling this world from Jerusalem?

What about that first moment of meeting Him face to face after death? There is a song by the group, Mercy Me[13] about this very happening. It is called 'I Can Only Imagine'. Check it out.

It never ceases to amaze me how God's written Word supports itself, is confirmed by history and archeological discoveries and has stood the test of time with people from all walks of life. Now it seems like Bible prophesy is written in today's news headlines.

I am confident in having Scripture, the Word of God, as a sure foundation for my life:

> *Thy word is a lamp unto my feet, and a light*
> *unto my path. (Psalm 119.105)*

THE MESSAGE OF this book, the Bible, is as applicable today as it was when the first part (Old Testament) was written and then the second part (New Testament) 2,000 years ago: we are all sinners, God had a plan to come to earth in the form of the man Jesus to rescue us.

It is a story of man's heart response to God because this is what He desires and, even when we don't recognise it, it is our deepest heart desire to be with Him

Prophecies in this book have been and continue to be fulfilled.

When Jesus walked the earth over 2,000 years ago, about 300 of the prophecies in the Bible are said to have been fulfilled.

Many have been killed in extreme ways because of the Bible and their belief in the God of the Bible.

WORDS OF SCRIPTURE have been a solace for many.

IT IS A STORY of relationship not ritual!

IT IS A STORY of the freedom of man to chose!

FROM GENESIS WE learn about the beginning.

IN REVELATION WE are told what is to come and how the story ends.

GRATITIUDE

I am thankful to have been blessed with many friends and Bible Study cohorts who have put up with my ramblings and questioning as I've journeyed the road of faith.

Especially, I am thankful for the many who have given their lives, many literally, as martyrs in order to preserve, translate, print and spread this amazing story; those who suffered and faced death because of their conviction of the truth of this relationship with a Heavenly God; and those who, over the years have studied this Book, the history of the times in which it was written, the ancient languages and then shared their learning and knowledge with us.

References

1. Bible quotes from the KJV from 'The Blue Letter Bible' https://www.blueletterbible.org/

2. Catechism published by ST PAULs - Society of St Paul Homebush NSW 1994

3. RJ Thesman, R. J. Can Loved Ones in Heaven Look Down on Me? https://www.crosswalk.com/faith/spiritual-life/can-loved-ones-in-heaven-look-down-on-me.html

4. Raymond Ibrahim (2018) Sword & Scimitar. De Capo Press, New York

5. The Book on the Virtues of Jihad https://www.islamicfinder.org/hadith/tirmidhi/virtues-of-jihad/?page=5

6. Jewish Virtual Library The Crusades. 1095 - 1291. https://www.jewishvirtuallibrary.org/the-crusades

7. Church teaching on Limbo https://www.reuters.com/article/us-pope-limbo/catholic-church-buries-limbo-after-centuries-idUSL2028721620070420

8. The Love of God. https://www.hymnal.net/en/hymn/h/28 1951 by Hope Publishing Co., Carol Stream, IL 60188.

9. William P. Welty, Ph.D., Mary (2016), Koinonia House, Coeur d'Alene, Idaho.

10. The Real Story of Fatima John de Marchi, I.M.C. https://fatima.org/wp-content/uploads/2017/03/The-True-Story-of-Fatima.pdf

11. Amazon Synod (2019) https://www.catholicnewsagency.com/news/pope-francis-apologizes-that-amazon-synod-figures-were-thrown-into-tiber-river-46833

12. Who is Pachamama? https://www.google.com/search?client=firefox-b-d&q=who+is+Pachamama

13. Mercy Me, I Can Only Imagine. https://mercyme.org/

* Nehushtan of copper; a brazen thing a name of contempt given to the serpent Moses had made in the wilderness (Numbers 21:8), and which Hezekiah destroyed because the children of Israel began to regard it as an idol and "burn incense to it." The lapse of nearly one thousand years had invested the "brazen serpent" with a mysterious sanctity; and in order to deliver the people from their infatuation, and impress them with the idea of its worthlessness, Hezekiah called it, in contempt, "Nehushtan," a brazen thing, a mere piece of brass (2 Kings 18:4).

https://www.biblestudytools.com/dictionary/nehushtan/

Printed in the United States
By Bookmasters